CONISBROUGH

A JOURNEY
THROUGH TIME

By Penny Lloyd-Rees

Illustrations by Mick Daines

Preface and Acknowledgements

While researching this book I wondered "where do I start?" I knew I wanted to look at the possible advent of the village of Conisbrough but the more I researched the earlier it appeared!

Hopefully, by starting at the very beginning, using archaeological evidence as clues to its origins, we can begin to appreciate the weight of history behind the lovely village that we see today.

Some of the history of the castle and its inhabitants has been well documented. Sharon Bennett-Connelly has written some excellent books on the De Warennes, which I highly recommend if you want to read about them in more depth, after you have read this book. The English Heritage guidebook also contains a wealth of information on the castle's history and construction.

I will be concentrating mostly on the stories through the ages; how world and countrywide events affected the whole village, and the everyday realities of living in a village like this.

Many thanks to the Heritage Lottery Fund whose grant has allowed me to spend time on writing this book and afford to publish it; my lovely proof reader Mark Wilson from English Heritage who has had to put up with strange questions such as "So– you've gone on Crusade with your lord and he's dropped off a mountain– do you a) Go native and settle down in a foreign country; b) Stay with the crusade under another lord or c) Have to make your own way home?" (Still waiting for the answer to that one!); Author Sharon Bennett-Connelly and Doncaster Archivist Charles Kelham for their constant encouragement and belief in me; Christine Eames from the local archaeology and research group CRAG, who generously handed over all her accumulated research of Conisbrough which was a price-less resource, especially with Doncaster Archives out of action for the main part of the research period, Benny Wilkinson for supplying the postscript in his own unique style, and last but definitely not least, Mick Daines, local cartoonist, whose ability to imagine scenes from the past and pull out the funnier elements makes the book an enjoyable read and not just a list of dry historical facts!

As usual when researching a book like this there are conflicting accounts from different sources. I have endeavoured to take them all into account and hopefully settle on the correct facts, though I foresee many a lively debate with our local historians in the future!

Penny Lloyd-Rees

Cover Illustration by Mick Daines

Other illustrations:
12th Century church and St George stone courtesy of South Yorkshire Archaeology Service

Contents

Where it all began

The earliest evidence we have of pre-historic life along the Don Valley was the discovery of Ice Age animal bones in the 1870s. Workmen digging a channel in the limestone crags near to a railway tunnel between Conisbrough and Sprotbrough found a femur, radius, tibia and shaft of humorous from a woolly rhinoceros; a metacarpal of a horse and a tibia of a Mammoth. It is thought that the bones were washed down from a cave further up the valley when it collapsed. The bones had been gnawed by hyenas in an age when the temperature was rarely above freezing and early man existed in the valley, before the last ice-age beat them back into Southern Europe. Our landscape at this time was a desolate, barren wilderness.

It was the final retreat of the ice sheets and the warming of the climate which led to humans returning to the area from 450,000 BCE. The Don Gorge changed from a treeless icy landscape to a wooded wonderland, and, as more animals moved in to the area, so did man. The British Isles were still physically connected to the continent by a land bridge, though Palaeolithic hunter gatherers may not have come this far north due to the ice sheets. By Mesolithic times from 10,000 BCE they would have been moving around the landscape taking advantage of natural resources, journeying mostly along the river valleys to make the most of natural harvests from season to season. Evidence of this nomadic lifestyle has been found on Cadeby Cliff where there have been many finds from this period including: flint microliths, used as the tips and barbs of arrows; awls, which when twisted, drilled holes; pieces of jet and bone knife handles, and scrapers, used for removing hair and fat from animal hides. Sites like the one on Cadeby Cliff with large amounts of scrapers are thought to have been used as seasonal base camps.

A number of high status flint objects were manufactured in the Neolithic period, examples of which have been found on the surface of ploughed fields in this same area, including arrowheads and a blade fragment from a flint axe with a polished blade. Not occurring in this area, the majority of flint is from the Yorkshire or Lincolnshire Wolds. Flint would also have been found on chalk coasts as pebbles, collected from beaches and traded locally. All in all, the Don valley would have been an ideal location to fish, hunt wild animals and forage for food on the grasslands above the gorge during the summer, before moving to the coast for the winter.

By the late Mesolithic, with warmer conditions prevailing, much of the area would have been wooded, though natural clearance through fire or wind damage would have kept some parts relatively open for a few crops to be grown on a seasonal basis.

The warmer climatic period extended into the Early Neolithic, when important changes began to take place. The Magnesian Limestone Plateau acted as a draw for organised communities, as a new population of farmers settled down, living in ditched and banked enclosures.

In the Pastures area of Mexborough there is an area of enclosures, trackways and field boundaries. On a hilltop overlooking the Dearne there was a group of two or three linked enclosures with a   potential roundhouse in one. One of the trackways descended east-wards to lower ground on the edge of the Dearne floodplain, and a series of ruts and hollows in between the trackway ditches suggest that there had been considerable movement along it by people, animals and potentially even wheeled vehicles.

Though most evidence of pre-historic life has been found on the south facing side of the Don Gorge taking advantage of the summer sunshine, Conisbrough, overlooking the river valley, could have had a similar settlement. Ten worked flints found in the Wellgate area seem to support this theory, with a scraper found elsewhere in the village.

This settling down period continued into the Bronze Age, an era also known for its barrows. In these huge earth mounds, chambers were constructed in which bodies were buried, together with food, vessels, ornaments and implements. Two of these large burial mounds have been identified in Sprotbrough at Scabba Wood and Melton Warren, between High Melton and Barnburgh.

On the Cadeby side of the valley, several springs emerge, which would have been useful for people living in the caves and rock shelters. They may also have been significant at this time on a spiritual level, as water was often seen as being sacred. Some of the steep valley slopes would have been wooded, as many are today, and would have created a slightly isolated, mysterious, or even other-worldly feel to the area.

The discovery of finds at Scabba Wood rock shelter seem to collaborate this theory, indicat-ing veneration of a site over thousands of years; as, in addition to late Neolithic and Bronze Age finds, Roman coins were located in the same area. Metal scabbard fittings from the late Iron Age were also found in the gorge, thought to have been left as a ritual offering in the first century CE.

 The population of Britain was growing during the Iron Age, made possible partly by the introduction of new crops, including improved varieties of barley and wheat, and increased farming of peas, beans, flax and other crops. Agriculture would have been the main activity on the local limestone plateau, due to the fertile well drained soils.

By the late Iron Age rivers were used as modes of transport themselves, but their valley floors were also used for pathways, following the course of the river. Surveying the land from the air has shown areas of fields and settlements, defined by ditches, enclosures and trackways. One of these types of trackway has been found in Conisbrough, and an enclosure in Denaby.

Artefacts found in the area are not necessarily made by local craftsmen, but often originate outside the area, proving that trade was emerging along these routes as settlements grew.

Roman Times

The 1,100 years folowing the Roman invasion of Britain was the most formative period in British history, when the country experienced several waves of invasion. Different cultures met and clashed time after time, permanently changing how people lived and worshipped. The British people worshiped Celtic pagan gods at the start of the period but became mostly Christians at its end. It is in this time that organised civilisation began with laws and treaties and land ownership becoming more formal than in the past.

The period both begins and ends with a major invasion: the first Roman invasion in 55 BCE and the Norman invasion of William the Conqueror in 1066 and in between were the Anglo-Saxon and Viking invasions.

The region either side of the River Don would have been a frontier zone from at least the late Iron Age onwards because the river was a physical boundary for the tribes of the Brigantes to the north of the river, and the Corieltauvi to the south. The area was important because it held the ancient river crossing at Strafforth Sands, situated somewhere between today's Mexborough and Conisbrough.

The powerful Celtic Brigantes territory spanned all of the north of England, except Humberside which was ruled by the Parisii. The Brigantes seem to have been a collection of tribes that either took their name from the Celtic goddess Brigantia who they are thought to have worshipped, or from their settlements which were mostly in the form of small hill crofts, the Celtic word "briga" meaning hill.

In 43 CE, when the leaders of a number of important British tribes met Roman Emperor Claudius, several of the tribes in the south of the country entered into a very close relationship with the Romans, taking on their customs and style of living.

I say scruff, you have been invaded by us Romans and if you don't do as you are told you'll receive a sound thrashing , Capeesh?

The Brigantes in the north though remained in control of their lands and people, and only used Roman support when necessary. For this support the Brigantes paid the Romans taxes, initially in slaves, hunting dogs and horses but eventually in coin.

The Celtic tribe of the Corieltauvi were, like their Brigantes neighbours to the north, a collection of smaller tribes who were mostly farmers and fairly unwarlike. Their territory stretched from modern day Leicestershire, through Nottinghamshire to Lincolnshire and included lower South Yorkshire. The Corieltauvi were also traders and minted coins inscribed with their leader's names for trading, but there is little evidence of their use around Doncaster. Romans also used money but it is likely that its uptake in this area would have been fairly slow.

Although the first Roman invasion of Britain by Julius Caesar was in 55 BCE the Romans did nothing more until 43 CE when the Emperor Claudius landed near to present day Colchester and began a systematic conquest of the land. Soon Roman armies had advanced as far north as the river Don and established defensive forts at Bawtry, Doncaster, Rossington, Burghwallis and Templeborough. There was a major Roman road from Birmingham to Buroughbridge via Templeborough; another route from Templeborough along the Roman Ridge to the north of Barnburgh which runs to Castleford, and a presumed road from Templeborough to Doncaster. Conisbrough lies on the direct route between these last two locations and it is likely that a road linking the two ran through or near to Conisbrough. The route of Old Road, West Street and Old Hill, to the crossing of the brook and a continuation along Doncaster Road and Drake Head Lane, is a good contender for the course of this road. Roman coins found in and around the village including those issued by emperors in the first century CE and the later horde forty coins from the Byzantine Roman Empire not far from Old Road also suggests that this may have been the route it took.

A Roman villa has been identified to the south of Old Road's junction at Hill Top which could be when the medieval hunting area that is still known as Conisbrough Parks was first formed. The park boundary comes close to three settlements: Clifton, on the eastern boundary, Firsby to the west and Micklebring to the south.

More locally, Carleton Henry Allport, an enthusiastic local historian writing at the beginning of the 20th century, says that there was a Roman road which came through Conisbrough from Cusworth, where there was a Roman colony and the Crispin Horse was stationed. He traces the road from Cusworth to Sprotbrough and then to the Kings Ferry in Conisbrough via Cadeby and on to Strafford Sands to Mexborough and Swinton where the northern Roman road mentioned above crossed to go to Castleford. He also tells of a Roman road or track which stretched across Northcliffe Hill which was still visible in his time, from which he says the Romans would have a clear view of the river valley and easy communication with Cusworth via watch towers or beacons. The ancient track to old Denaby could be a part of this roadway which Allport tells us of. The Conisbrough map of 1854 shows this feature as a footpath along the ridge of the hill.

Through the centuries all traces of these roads have been removed due to the reusing of their materials, ploughing or building developments. In some instances all that remains of a Roman road is a wide shallow trench or the paved foundation a foot or more below the modern day level of the ground. Intriguingly the footpath down to Old Denaby has areas of paving or cobbling along it which could be the remains of a Roman road.

Some Celts learnt the language of their invaders, and adapted to their way of life, but in the Conisbrough area it seems that, although there were definitely Romans around, the general population and how they lived were not changed by their presence. In fact, life for ordinary farming people in Roman Yorkshire was far less influenced by the occupation than further south, where large slave-run farms provided huge amounts of grain for the army.

Field systems remained much the same as before, though field markings show that some may have expanded to provide extra income for the farmers selling to the passing Roman soldiers; and traditional round houses, some of them hundreds of years old, remained in use.

In Conisbrough parish itself, a few items of Roman culture have been found but no village or farm sites are known apart from the Roman settlement at Hill Top. However, during the excavations at Wellgate, there were archaeological remains dating from the Roman period onwards including Roman pottery made between the first and fourth centuries CE, along with other evidence of settlement nearby during the Roman period. In the south porch of the church is a piece of well weathered Romano-British carving thought to be either the Virgin and Child or St Peter with the key of Heaven. One of the pillars at the back of the north arcade is thought to be a bit of recycled Roman masonry from a nearby villa, with the figures of Roman soldiers depicted on it.

Of the few villas built in the area there is little evidence that Roman goods like glass, kitchen ware and amphorae found their way to the native peoples. Even the mosaic floors that survive are crude country versions of the ones in southern villas.

Other evidence of the Romans in and around the village come from a few scraps of Roman pottery that were discovered on the Crags and a Hadrian coin found in the castle grounds.

Slightly further afield, the Cadeby hoard of Roman coins and bracelets was found on the Don Valley walls in Pot Ridings Wood, part of Sprotbrough Flash, in 1981. The hoard was found in a natural fissure in the limestone rock that had been capped with a limestone slab. Within this was a small 'poppy' ceramic jar containing 112 denarii and antoniniani dating to 194-251 CE, and four silver bracelets. One pair of the bracelets was set with cornelians and the other pair were 'snake' bracelets. Snakes and snake bracelets were known for their religious symbolism with possible associations with Mercury, god of travellers and commerce, Asclepios, god of healing or Glycon the hunter god, which implies that the hoard was left as an offering rather than hidden for safe keeping, and that the area was still seen as sacred.

Edlington Wood has a Roman settlement, with the pottery, coin and metalwork found there suggesting that there was at least one relatively high-status settlement belonging to either a successful 'native' farmstead that thrived during the Roman occupation, or perhaps a Roman settler living there.

During the Roman period many of the existing Celtic leaders had been allowed to enjoy their former rights and jurisdictions, in exchange for paying a tribute to the Roman Empire. In return, the Romans had repelled the Anglo-Saxon invaders from Germany and the Low Countries, but in 410 when the last of the Roman army left Britain, its inhabitants were left alone to face the new wave of invaders and without the Roman reinforcement the Anglo-Saxons gradually moved in.

The Battle of Maes Beli

This next chapter of our history has been difficult to research. Far from the reassuring certainty of archaeological finds and eons of time covered in which to work with, the period after the Romans retreated back to their Mediterranean roots is not well documented, and when it is, it seems that no contemporary historian has the same account of events which presumably did happen.

At a time where history was mainly passed down through generations by word of mouth rather than written down, histories were sometimes not recorded until a couple of centuries after the fact and each author wrote from his own, often biased, perspective, so that modern day researchers have to weigh up each account and try to reach a happy medium. Histories started to be written from the end of the fifth century by Gildas, and in the eighth century by Bede, and many Anglo-Saxon histories are based on their works.

Gildas, a monk thought to have lived in the south west of England, is not thought of as a reliable source for events in the north of the country. His main work *'De excidio Britonum'* 'On the Ruin of Britain' wasn't so much a history as a moral lecture, as he criticises his British kings for their unholy behaviour, which he believed brought the Saxon invasion upon Britain as divine judgment. Gildas often omits names, but he does include events which took place. In fact the only fifth century figure he does name is Ambrosius Aurelianus, a historical figure who is found on record from other sources, and the hero of our upcoming tale.

The Venerable Bede lived in a Northumbrian monastery in the eighth century and is considered relatively reliable for recording northern events when compared with other sources from his time. Most of Bede's work though, concerning the fifth and sixth centuries, seems to have been taken from Gildas but was later edited, and it fills in many names. Historians believe that he must have had access to some other writings, now lost to us, for this edit.

Bede's best known book is *'Historia Ecclesiastica Gentis Anglorum'* 'Ecclesiastical History of the English People' in which we find the story of King Vortigern and how he brought in the Saxons Horsa and Hengist, to fight as mercenaries for him. In Bede's account, the Saxons always intended to betray the Britons and join forces with the Picts, but, as mentioned before, this kind of bias is rife in writings from the period.

The Anglo-Saxon Chronicle, a series of chronicles covering all aspects of Anglo-Saxon times, is another piece of work from the ninth century but containing information of earlier periods, which helps put people and events in context. These annals recorded information on a variety of subjects, from major battles and Viking invasions, to information of the deaths of notable people from across Britain.

Many of the ancient history stories and legends we know of today though are from a rather flamboyant author Geoffrey of Monmouth, who enthusiastically pulled stories and characters together and added pieces here and there for dramatic effect. The 'History of Kings' written by Geoffrey in 1136 was supposedly based on 'Britannica Sermonis Librum Uetustissimum' 'The British Book of the Old History' an ancient book never seen by any of his contemporaries, but supposedly supplied to him by Walter, Archdeacon of Oxford. His histories include many tales around the Arthurian legends, but also the story of a famous battle which concerns our local area!

Writing at a similar time as Geoffrey was Henry of Huntingdon, whose most notable work was the *'Historia Anglorum'* the 'History of the English'. He was tasked by Bishop Alexander of Lincoln to write a history of England from its earliest period and bring it to 'modern times' ending with the accession of Henry II in 1154. He based his earlier histories on the 'Anglo-Saxon Chronicle' as mentioned above, written between the ninth and twelfth centuries and as such is regarded as a more reliable source than Geoffrey of Monmouth's, though not nearly as entertaining!

The story which we will be looking at is that of the Battle of Maes Beli in 487 CE relying on Geoffrey's account for the battle details. The area of Maes Beli is thought to be around the Denaby/Mexborough Ings area.

The Romans had dominated the country for 320 years and following their departure, with no one to defend it, it became a hotbed for infighting, with local tribes vying for supremacy and constant raids from the Picts and Scots. High-King Constantine ruled England but when he was murdered by Pictish assassins, one of the British tribal leaders, Vortigern, saw to it that Constantine's eldest son, Constans, rule in his stead with Vortigern as his chief advisor. When the teenage Constans was murdered Vortigern seized the throne.

Ambrosius Aurelianus, the second son of Constantine, was a young boy when his brother's reign came to its sudden end. With his father executed and his brother murdered, Ambrosius and his brother Uther, were taken across the Channel to the court of their cousin, Budic I of Brittany.

Unfortunately for Vortigern, with the unrest throughout Britain and invaders causing even more havoc, he had to resort to drastic measures in order to quell the unrest. He invited the Saxon brothers Hengist and Horsa, to protect his kingdom against the Picts and Scots and rewarded them for their services with grants of land in Kent, Essex and Sussex.

Hengist is featured heavily in Geoffrey's tale. He, along with Vortigern is alleged to have invited all of the British Leaders to a peace treaty on the Hill of Ambrius near Salisbury in 456 CE. Due to the nature of the event all parties were told to come unarmed. Hengist though had ordered his men to come with knives in their boots, and when all of the elders were assembled, about 460 in total, Hengist ordered his men to draw their knives and kill them all, in a massacre known as the 'Night of the Long Knives'. The invention of one survivor of the slaughter, Eldol, Duke of Gloucester plays a major part in Geoffrey's tale. According to Geoffrey of Monmouth, Eldol survived Hengist's massacre by grabbing a stick and killing seventy men as he escaped.

Meanwhile Romano-Briton Ambrosius had returned to Britain and already started to claim his rightful inheritance. He landed on the south coast and waged war on King Vortigern. After some victories he was "given all the kingdoms of the western side of Britain" but, not satisfied with this compromise he started building up support in a bid to control the whole country.

Vortigern's pro-Saxon policies eventually led to his downfall with even his sons rebelling against him, and in the late 450s, possibly partly due to the massacre, the British people finally rallied behind Ambrosius Aurelius to rid them of their Anglo-Saxon oppressors. During this on-going warfare with Ambrosius, Vortigern was hounded into taking refuge in one of his mountain strongholds in Wales. While under siege the fortress was 'miraculously' struck by lightning (or Ambrosius set fire to the fortress as other sources report!) and Vortigern and his entire garrison were burnt to death.

Eldol was understandably a key supporter of Aurelius Ambrosius and intent on exacting revenge on Hengist and helping him defeat the Saxons. He is thought to have been at the siege of Vortigern's Welsh fortress. Ambrosius allowed Vortigern's sons to keep their lands, but despite this they later rebelled against Ambrosius and twice attempted to over-run Britain with help from the Saxons and the Irish.

After the death of Vortigern, Ambrosius turned his attention to Hengist's hold on the north of Britian. The leaders of the Brigantes had obtained his services to lead them against the Saxons. It is said that the Saxons had already heard of Ambrosius' bravery and battle prowess so they retreated beyond the Humber to gather a massive army to face the Britons. According to some accounts Hengist's army consisted of 200,000 men. Ambrosius had the help of Eldol the Duke of Gloucester, Eldad, the Bishop of Gloucester, and numer-ous others, but his army numbered only 10,000.

Hengist had seized the fortress at Conisbrough as his base and intended to be in the field of Maes Beli to face the army of Britons when they arrived. But Ambrosius had been tipped off and got to the battle site first, causing Hengist to march his army over the Strafford Sands river crossing to meet them. Ambrosius had his Britons organised into cavalry, archers and pikes/lances, sticking to Roman tactics. The Saxons attacked with their short swords, charging in one dense column, but after much bloodshed they were eventually defeated. Some were unable to escape and cross the River Don, and were chased along the northern bank of the Don to Sprotbrough, while others were driven back towards Conisbrough. Ambrosius pursued them; apparently killing or forcing into slavery every man he overtook on the way.

When Hengist saw that Ambrosius was following him, he decided not to retreat back to the fortress at Conisbrough, knowing that the only defence left to him was in a second battle. He once more drew up his soldiers into their ranks, arranging them so that they were ready to join battle again. When Ambrosius had caught up with him, he also ranked his soldiers in formation, and charged on the enemy. The Saxons held their ground, and both sides had great losses.

The second battle was more evenly fought, and Hengist would have had a chance to achieve victory, had a company of mounted knights of the Armorican Britons not joined the fight. Ambrosius had stationed them apart, as he had done in the first battle for such an occasion, and when the Armoricans charged down upon them, the Saxons were forced to give ground, and once broken were not able to form up again.

Eldol, who had vowed vengeance on Hengist for the massacre of the elders, met Hengist in single combat in this second battle. He took Hengist by the nasale of his helmet, and dragged him from his men, who were by then entirely routed.

Ambrosius, having won the second battle, took Conisbrough and stayed there for three days. He ordered the dead to be buried and the wounded to be taken care of. There next became the question of what should be done with Hengist.

Without hesitation Eldol took control of the situation, and taking up his sword, he led Hengist outside and cut off his head. Aurelius ordered Hengist to be buried and a barrow of earth to be raised over his body, adhering to the pagan custom.

The history continues to relate how Ambrosius then led his army to York where Octa, Hengist's son, with the greater part of the remaining Saxon army, had made its way. Eosa, Hengist's kinsman, had made for the city of Dumbarton, and garrisoned himself there with a small army. Both these surviving Saxon leaders readily submitted themselves to Ambrosius' rule. He pardoned them and granted them an area of land in the far north.

The 'Historia Brittonum' by ninth century historian Nennius also records the massacre of the British nobles and Vortigern's subsequent grant of lands in Essex and Sussex to the Saxon invaders.

From the Anglo-Saxon Chronicle we learn that Hengist and Horsa, came into England in 449 CE. We have accounts of various transactions concerning them which brought their history to the year 473. From that time we hear no more of Hengist; where or how he died, though when his history is dropped by the Chronicle, he was engaged in active warfare with the Britons away from his base in Kent. The year 488 is assigned as the date of his successor Esc.

Geoffrey of Monmouthshire's major character is Hengist, leader of the Saxons. Other Saxon characters receive less attention from him, but their names do correspond to Anglo-Saxons known from other sources. Hengist's supposed son Octa is apparently Octa of Kent, a sixth century ruler connected to Hengist either as a son or other descendant. The other kinsman Eosa is more difficult to identify.

Geoffrey of Monmouthshire contemplating his histories

Rev Joseph Hunter an historian in the 19th century, writing on Geoffrey's account of the battle states "I shall just observe upon this part of the narrative, that this account of the pursuit is scarcely consistent with the belief that by Maisbeli Jeffery intended those level lands on the left bank of the Don between Coningsborough and Mexborough, for if that had been the scene of the battle there would have been but a very short pursuit of the flying army".

"Near the castle wall is a mound of earth, but now scarcely to be discerned, called Hengist's Tomb, which is maintained to be the identical tumulus which Jeffery informs us was raised over the body of Hengist. This is no modern invention, for it is so denominated by Camden. If tradition has faithfully carried down the occasion of the throwing up this green mound, the question of the death of Hengist may be considered as settled. But it may be that some person has led the people of Coningsborough to annex this name to the mound, having himself read of the event in the pages of Jeffery".

When Matthew of Westminster tells this same story, he makes an interval of two years between the first and second fight. He says "The battle occurred in 487 at a plain called Maes Beli. Aurelius defeated the whole united force of the Saxons who first meant to surprise the army of the Britons as they entred the plain. The slaughter on both sides was great but with the Saxons coming off worse. Hengist and his troops retreated to Conisbrough but continued to fight rather than be beleaguered in the fortress there. The Britons followed, beheading all the fugitives they overtook on the road". The story of Hengist being captured and beheaded seems to have followed this defeat though Matthew consigns it to happening two years later in 489. He states that Ambrosius compelled Octa and Eosa to submit in 490 so that the battle didn't conclude until this year. In other respects Matthews's account agrees with Geoffrey's and uses Geoffrey's own words, though he consigns the handy arrival of the Amoric horsemen to another battle with Ambrosius.

I found speculation elsewhere that the battle took place somewhere rather closer to Sheffield than Mexborough, which would perhaps make better sense of the battle account. If the initial battle did take place somewhere along the old Roman road from Sheffield, which is a route that Ambrosius could have taken to get to Hengist while he was encamped at Conisbrough, then it makes sense that Hengist would have fled that battle and headed back to Conisbrough, only to realise that he wasn't going to be able to defend the fortress and therefore rally his troops in the area that we know as Maes Beli for the second battle.

Anglo-Saxon Period

The period of history after the Romans had left our shores used to known as the Dark Ages, a time when there was little cultural advancement and its people were unsophisticated and unruly. In fact the Anglo-Saxons established a lot of how we now live in Britain today. They spoke "Old English", and many of today's oldest English towns and villages have names going back to this era. Most Anglo-Saxons were pagan when they arrived, but many converted to Christianity and sent missionaries back to their homelands of Germany and the Low Countries.

Anglo-Saxon writings in Latin and Old English survive in religious texts; law codes; charters and writs; they also gave us the BC/AD method of dating. They were the first people to record the history of England in works such as the "Ecclesiastical History of the English People" and "The Anglo-Saxon Chronicle", and produce manuscripts illustrated in colour, including the Lindisfarne Gospels.

The Anglo-Saxons learnt from the Romans, and used their know-how for establishing their own central and local government along with taxation systems. People lived under a feudal system with peasants holding their land in exchange for services to their lord. Anglo-Saxon written laws and punishments formed the foundation for our modern legal system.

By 650 CE there were seven separate kingdoms in England: Kent; Mercia, which stretched over the Midlands; Northumbria; East Anglia, made up of Angles; Norfolk (the North Folk) and Suffolk (the South Folk); Essex (East Saxons); Sussex (South Saxons) and Wessex (West Saxons).

Conisbrough may have been a royal estate and minster for the Northumbrian or Mercian kings throughout the Anglo-Saxon period, sitting on the border of the two kingdoms and it seems to have been the most important place in South Yorkshire by the end of the period.

The name Conisbrough itself reflects its importance at this time, as it originates from the Anglo-Saxon Cyninges-burh, meaning 'the defended burh of the King'. Its position near the ford where a highway crossed the River Don meant that those who held Conisbrough would control local politics and trading routes connecting the South and the North of England. The name of the ancient ferry crossing over the Don, at the foot of the hill from Cadeby has passed through the centuries as the 'King's Ferry', but exactly which king is still a matter of speculation, though could have originated from this period.

King Ethelred reinforced local defences by building fortified townships known as burhs. Burh building was stepped up in the ninth century as the Viking threat increased. Like Conisbrough, Mexborough contains a later motte and bailey castle and was therefore probably a burh in Anglo-Saxon times. Other fortified burhs found along the Dearne/Don corridor include Sprotbrough, Barnburgh, Worsbrough, Masbrough and Greasbrough which formed the new Northumberland and Mercian border. Safety works on the outer bailey of the castle site revealed remains associated with this earlier timber fortress.

In Conisbrough there were extensive earthen walls forming the boundary of the village, surrounding the church and Wellgate area with the dominant family living in a large hall in the centre of the complex and the castle area providing a fortified lookout tower. The earthworks would also help prevent farm animals from straying and protect them from wolves. Local villagers would be obliged to work on these earthwork defences as part of their service to the local lord and would also have to defend the village when needed as part of the 'fyrd'.

During the early Anglo-Saxon period, most people would have lived in wooden framed huts, raised above the ground on stout wooden posts with wattle and daub walls. Roofs would have been made from reed thatch or wooden shingles. There would be no streets laid out -just a scattering of houses within the fortification.

Conisbrough Minster Church from Wellgate

Archaeological excavations in Wellgate uncovered a massive plank-walled construction dated by dendrochronology to the late sixth or early seventh century. It contained wooden structures including a fence; a line of stakes; a wooden box structure and a wattle track. It is possible that it formed the middle section of a long pond, at least 11m long by 7m wide, perhaps using the water from the spring for a fishpond or other agricultural function, such as wetting flax or hemp. If it was a fishpond it would fit in with the idea that there was an elite residence here possibly connected to the church. This area is the oldest part of the village and in 1936 when Conisbrough UDC embarked their slum clearance scheme they removed many old stone buildings from the area. It was noted that one of the buildings, a large house known as the Priory Manor, was of great historical value. Upon demolition, the house was found to have thick stone walls on the lower level with timber framing and wattle and daub on the upper level. This version of the building was thought to be dated to the six-teenth century but it has been suggested that it was built on or near the site of an earlier medieval manor house or even earlier structure. Although no remains of either building survive, a medieval well house still stands in Wellgate, which may have served the Priory Manor. Whatever the Conisbrough building was, it probably formed part of an important area with other elite buildings, either monastery or palace, close to the minster church.

Peter Langtoft, writing in the thirteenth century, says that King Egbert and his suite passed a Whitsuntide at Conisbrough in about 830, and other sources state that in 1022 King Malcolm of Scotland stayed at Priory Manor on his way to Worcester. These were the times when a king and his retinue would move around the country, living off his subjects' hospitality. The house stood close to the rear boundary wall of the shops on the lower part of Church Street and feeds in to the theory that there was a priory in Conisbrough associated with the church. Although the present building 'The Priory' wasn't built until the nineteenth century, it seems there was a small ancient chapel on the site, which may have caused the owners to presume it was a part of the older priory complex. The chapel could have been in the grounds, close to the stone wall of the pathway between High Street and Castle Avenue.

Further evidence of settlement elsewhere in the village in the fifth and sixth centuries includes a hoard of 40 Nummia coins from the Eastern Roman or Byzantine Empire found on Daylands Avenue. The 40 coins date from 527-565 during the reign of Justinian I.

Though the stone church was thought to have been built in around 750, two historic building archaeologists independent of each other have likened the masonry to that of St Peter's in Monkwearmouth which was built circa 680, stating that the same masons built both. In 664 CE Wulfhere, King of Mercia signed a confirmation and grant of land for the building of the church. It seems more plausible to have built the church within 20 years of the grant of land rather than nearly a century afterwards therefore the date may well be even earlier than previously thought.

From the foundation of the church the whole of the fee formed one great parish. Conisbrough was the Minster Church for a large area south of the Don to the borders of Hallamshire. In the Doncaster area, these included Warmsworth, Armthorpe, Braithwell, Fishlake, Hatfield, Kirk Sandall and Thorne, though during medieval times they all became separate parishes under the Clunic Abbey at Lewes.

Conisbrough still has the ancient pathway that people from Ravenfield, Hooten Roberts and other nearby villages used to follow to worship at St Peter's Church. The path can be followed from the bottom of Ellershaw Road past the cricket ground and parallel to Holywell Lane to the stone stile on Spring Grove, down the stone steps on to Chapel Lane and High Street to the Church.

The church that we know today holds the original Anglo-Saxon church as its nave. Evidence of the outer part of the building at this point in time is shown by knife marks on the wall, on the south-eastern aisle where people would sharpen their knives on the stonework before proceeding into church, and traces of window surrounds in the stonework.

The windows were small and high up in order to let light in without the building becoming too cold. These original stone windows can be seen on the north side of the central nave. The interior would have been dark and lit by candles. Another arched opening visible in this original wall would have been used for the vicar to look out over the church from his accommodation in the Porticus when the building on this side had two storeys. On the floor is an old tomb slab with two ravens carved on the top. The date is unknown but it could be Saxon, as ravens were a common symbol in Saxon heraldry.

The size and design of the church shows that it was never intended for a small and obscure manor, but for one of great importance where space was needed and money no object.

The churchyard was being used from the time it was built and evidence of an Anglo-Saxon burial was noted by historian Edward Miller in 1804 when he was overseeing an excavation at the church. He noted that "When the Norman tomb was moved, digging down revealed a north-south burial and directly under this which was clearly an east-west cist burial with charcoal." It is possible that the east-west burial was a late Anglo-Saxon charcoal burial and the north-south burial could be any date prior to the eighth century.

Vikings

Though sporadic raids were going on long before, the main Viking invasion period began in around 793 when they crossed the North Sea and attacked Northumbria at Lindisfarne; with the Vikings gradually taking control of parts of Britain up and down the North Sea coast. Once the Vikings had established themselves along the coasts they spread further inland along navigable rivers to build towns and villages; farming and trading along the River Humber.

In 867 two rival kings of Northumbria, Aelle and Osberht, joined forces against the invading Viking armies when they marched on York. The kings' efforts were in vain though and the Vikings seized the town, renaming it Jorvik. Jorvik remained their main base right up until the Norman Conquest, in 1066.

The Vikings proceeded to take over Northumbria, East Anglia and parts of Mercia. The kings of Mercia and Wessex resisted as best they could, but with little success until the time of Alfred 'the Great'. King Alfred defeated the Vikings at the Battle of Edington in 878 and in 886 took London from them, signing a treaty with the Viking leader Guthrum later the same year. The treaty divided England between Vikings and English. The north and east of the country became known as the Danelaw and was ruled by Danish Kings. The term Danelaw described both the territories that the Danes had power over and the laws with which they ruled.

With Danelaw came our modern shire counties such as York, Lancaster, Nottingham, Derby, Lincoln and Cambridge. They also divided Yorkshire into three Ridings; North, East and West. The new names and laws were eventually accepted as a part of the Anglo-Saxon-Danish legal system though in Danish legislation, punishments became more severe, including exile, mutilation, or death. Administrative areas started to take on Danish names, such as wapentakes, in the Danelaw. Wapentakes took over from the previous 'hundreds' which areas had previously been divided into. Conisbrough lay in the Strafforth Wapentake, named after the river crossing which was still an important place for chiefs to meet and hear disputes. The Strafford Wapentake was a large district on the upper Don and Dearne, including Darfield, Wombwell, Hoyland, Ecclesfield and Bradfield in the west. It was larger than the usual wapentake size but this can be explained by the natural terrain of the district: in the east were the Hatfield Moors and other marshy districts, and in the west it extended into the moorland of the Pennines.

The ninth century Anglo-Saxon Chronicle doesn't mention any Viking raids in this region, though they may have initially reached this far during the Viking incursions of the 870s to the East Midlands. The lasting Viking archaeological and landscape evidence tends to date to later decades, when Vikings began to establish themselves into many local areas, possibly peacefully.

It looks as though the fortified burhs established by Ethelred managed to keep their own identities, as the Viking settlers seem to be pushed into settlements just outside the Dearne and Don Valley, to places such as Maltby, Grimethorpe, Goldthorpe, Edenthorpe and Armthorpe, the suffix –by, meaning farm and –thorpe, meaning village in old Danish. Closer to home though, the settlements of Denaby and Cadeby both with Viking names, are located midpoint between the Mexborough and Conisbrough and Conisbrough and Sprotbrough fortifications. Nearby, Firsby means the farm of the Frisians, suggesting that these were all new farms created by these Viking settlers.

Er! J think we'll just stick to a bit of pillaging today Erik!

Many words in our language are Scandinavian in origin. Yorkshire people still use 'beck' instead of 'stream' and 'bairns' for children. Viking streets are called 'gates', and in Conisbrough we find Milnergate; Wellgate and Windgate which were all ancient routes to and from the village.

There is little cultural evidence of the Vikings in South Yorkshire, though a fragment of Anglo-Scandinavian sculpture with Ringerike style carving in St Peter's Church may be from a memorial set up by the descendent of one of these settlers, it being from the tenth century. An excavation of a woman buried with a range of Viking-style artefacts at Adwick-le -Street suggests that Vikings held on to their cultural identity. The woman's grave contained tortoiseshell brooches, a copper alloy bowl, an iron knife and a key.

In Anglo-Saxon times Conisbrough was an important religious site which had grown around the church of St Peter, but in the Viking era the power shifted to the castle outcrop as the fortified administrative centre of the Wapentake. A small amount of Anglo-Saxon pottery was recovered from the castle site, suggesting that the site was occupied for several centuries before the Norman Conquest. The pottery shards all come from a small jar made in North Lincolnshire between the ninth and eleventh centuries.

People had been building in timber for thousands of years and there was plenty of timber available to the Vikings. It is said that Vikings didn't like to live in old buildings so their timber houses were replaced around every twenty years. Usually all we can hope to find of an ancient timber building of this period is its foundations where posts and beams have rotted away, leaving marks in soil colour and texture. It wasn't possible to be sure what their buildings looked like above ground until excavations started in York, where special soil conditions preserved the foundation timbers of the buildings and the lower parts of the wooden walls, giving us a better knowledge of what Viking houses in England would have looked like.

The early tenth century houses in York had walls made of wattlework. Strong upright posts were set along the wattle walls to hold up a thatched roof. The floors were earth, with a large rectangular hearth in the middle, marked out with stone blocks, wooden beams or even old Roman tiles. The only trace of any furniture found was a pair of benches, made by piling up earth and turf against the wall, and then surrounding it with a low length of wattle-work. At the back of the houses were yards, wells, storage pits, rubbish pits and cesspits.

The Viking raids did not stop after Alfred and Guthrum's treaty and different Viking bands continued to make regular raiding voyages around the coasts of Britain. While King Alfred had conceded lands south of the Don, his successor Edward the Elder began to take back territories.

Alfred's grandson, Athelstan, became the first true King of England. He led the English to victory over the Vikings at the Battle of Brunaburh in 937, with his kingdom for the first time including the Danelaw. But as hostilities continued Conisbrough must have been at the heart of the conflict, until 954 when Eric Bloodaxe was killed in battle and his kingdom was taken over by English earls. Even so, peace was short-lived, as in 991, during the reign of King Ethelred; Olaf Tryggvason's Viking raiding party defeated the Anglo-Saxon defenders with Ethelred having to pay 'Danegeld' in an attempt to buy them off.

Even so the Vikings were not permanently defeated, and England was to have four Viking kings between 1013 and 1042. The greatest of these was King Cnut, who was king of Denmark as well as England. He did not force the English to obey Danish law; instead he recognised Anglo-Saxon law and customs. He worked to create a north Atlantic empire uniting Scandinavia and Britain. Unfortunately, he died at the age of 39 so his vision was never realised, and his sons had short, troubled reigns.

Wulfric Spot

In the midst of the struggles between the English and Vikings we have our first glimpse of who was the lord of Conisbrough- Wulfric Spot. It is thought that Wulfric Spot was born around 945 and probably lived in Wolverhampton, after his mother Wulfun was gifted the estate in 985 by King Ethelred. We can't be certain exactly when he died, but we do know for sure that he founded Burton Abbey at Burton on Trent as a Benedictine abbey.

From his will we know that Wulfric owned extensive estates in Mercia; Staffordshire; Derbyshire; Warwickshire and Northumbria. In the 'History of the Abbots', the monks at Burton refer to Wulfric as a councillor and thane of noble lineage. A thane was a person ranking between an earl and an ordinary freeman, holding land from the king in return for services. Wilfric witnessed many important charters of King Ethelred's time and many documents include his brother Alfhelm and Alfhelm's son, Wulfheah as signatories.

Wulfric comes into our story when he left Conisbrough in his will in the care of Alfhelm who was also charged with looking after Wulfric's only daughter. In his will he states: "And I grant to Alfhelm the estate at Cunugesburh, on condition that he arrange that the monks [At Burton Abbey] shall have each year a third of the fish, and he two thirds. And I grant to my wretched daughter the estate at Elleforda and that at Acclea, with all that now belongs there as long as her life lasts, and after her death the land is to go the monastery at Burton. And she shall not possess it on such terms that she can forfeit it for any reason, but she is to have the use of it as long as she can perform the services due from it, and afterwards it is to go to the monastery at Burton because it was my godfather's gift. And I desire that Alfhelm may be the protector of her and of the land."

Goodness me Brother Ignatecous, whence did thou last take a bath?

Wulfric himself seems to have had no sons, as the only child mentioned in the will was his 'wretched daughter'. It is thought that she may have been an invalid or disabled in some way, and was possibly living in a religious community.

It is thought that the fish mentioned in the will would not have come from Conisbrough itself but from Fishlake and Hatfield where there were vast fisheries under Conisbrough's domain.

The actual date of Wulfric Spot's death is uncertain. He may have died shortly after he made his will, sometime between 1002 when he is last recorded as a witness to a charter of King Ethelred, and 1004 when the charter which contains a copy of the will was confirmed by Ethelred at his Christmas court. But a tradition survived at Burton, and is recorded in the 'History of the Abbots', that Wulfric actually died on 22nd October 1010, fighting the Danes at Ipswich; though if this was so, he would have had to rewrite his will, as his brother had died some years before. He is said to have been buried at Burton under a stone arch next to the lower door of the church, beside his wife Ealhswith.

Wulfric's brother Alfhelm became ealdorman of Northumbria in the 990s and as such would have led his men in battle, presided over courts and levied taxes on his subjects. Ealdormanries were the possession of noble families and semi-independent rulers, and he was important enough that his third child, a daughter called Alfgifu, married King Cnut.

Unfortunately Alfhelm was murdered in 1006 by one of King Ethelred's supporters and his sons blinded. It is not known if this was as a direct request from Ethelred, but we do know that Ethelred had lost the allegiance of many of his subjects as he tried to defend the land against the Viking raiders, buying them off with money derived from the unpopular Danegeld taxes. Ethelred later took the Duke of Normandy's daughter Emma, as his second wife, which may be why, 60 years later, their great nephew, William, Duke of Normandy felt that he had a right to the English throne.

At some point, probably after the death of Alfhelm's sons, Conisbrough reverted back to the crown and found itself in the ownership of Earl Harold- soon to become King Harold, by the time of the Norman invasion of 1066. It is thought that Earl Harold resided in Conisbrough, possibly at the Priory Manor in Wellgate at this time and the first alteration of the church in 1050 was probably done under his instruction. The north side of the church was extended from the porticus and lateral chamber to a northern aisle with three arches, by taking down the internal walls, and the chancel was enlarged. On one of the columns the masons installed a Roman carved column capitol probably from a nearby villa. The carving, which has been vandalised by seventeenth century Puritan iconoclasts, shows Roman soldiers – one whose arm seems to be being eaten by a serpent.

Later Viking period and 1066

After the death of Cnut's son and successor, Harthacnut, the kingdom went back to a Saxon king, Edward the Confessor. But when Edward the Confessor ascended to the throne of the united Dano-Saxon England, every Norwegian colony in the British Isles raised an army and attacked him in support of Norway's Magnus Olavsson, who had been promised the throne by Harthacnut after his death. Even when Magnus died, his brother Harald Hardrada took over the claim to the English throne.

In early 1066 King Edward died and the nobleman Harold Godwinson took over the English crown.

King Harold made his brother Tostig earl of Northumbria, but Tostig was so unpopular that the Northumbrian thanes refused to serve him. He was replaced by Earl Morcar, helped by another Northumbrian earl, Edwin.

Tostig escaped to Flanders which was friendly to Duke William of Normandy, returning to England with a fleet to plunder along the south coast; but Harold's army and navy were on high alert, and repelled him. Tostig then sailed up the east coast, and tried plundering Northumbria, but was repelled again, this time by Edwin and Morcar, and he fled to Scotland with his supporters.

Harold used up a lot of time and resources through the summer of 1066 dealing with Tostig. Eventually though he had to disband his fleet and send his part-time warriors, the 'fyrd', home to bring in the harvest.

On 8th September news reached Harold that Tostig was back yet again. This time Tostig had managed to get help from Scotland and the king of Norway, Harald Hardrada, who was still pursuing his claim to the English throne. Together, they had sailed up the river Humber and were heading for York, plundering as they went.

Harold immediately set off from London with his Housecarles, his small permanent professional army, and as many men as he could find who hadn't yet gone home.

Earls Edwin and Morcar meanwhile had formed an army together and confronted Tostig and Hardrada two miles outside York at Gate Fulford. In this battle, on 20th September, the English were routed and the earls were forced back to York, which was then taken. On 25th September, while they were deciding the terms of peace, King Harold arrived.

Hardrada's Viking army, resting at Stamford Bridge on the River Derwent, was taken completely by surprise. A few of them hurried to defend the bridge, while the rest of the army struggled to get into position. The bridge was stormed, and Harold's men broke through. The Vikings defended themselves as well as they could but both Hardrada and Tostig were killed, the Vikings routed, and the handful of survivors were granted safe passage home.

Numbers of those involved in the two battles are not known, but it is thought there may have been seven or eight thousand on each side. Ordericus Vitalis, a Norman chronicler writing over fifty years later, spoke of heaps of bones still littering the battlefield.

News now came to Harold that another invasion force was in imminent danger of landing on the south coast, and with no time to rest after his victory, Harold's army travelled swiftly south to meet this new threat. His route is not known and there is speculation whether he went on foot; took advantage of the fleet of Viking war ships now abandoned in the Humber estuary, or marched to the River Trent to sail to London by the 6th October. He may have even paused at Conisbrough to regroup on his way, but there wouldn't have been much time in which to do so. William, Duke of Normandy, had decided to take the crown of England, and his invasion fleet landed at Pevensey on 28th September 1066, whether as part of an overall plan devised alongside Hardrada's invasion in the north, or as an unhappy coincidence, we may never know. By the 29th September William was occupying Hastings and had time to look over potential battlefields before Harold and his army arrived overnight on 13/14th October.

Hey Young Man, stop waving that Bow about– You might hit someone in the eye!

Despite the time William had to prepare, Harold's position was strong, and when William attacked the English gave no ground. It was in fact the Norman army which broke first in the belief that William had been killed, but the Duke rallied his troops and attacked again. It was later, when the Normans feigned retreat, that the English were lured away from their defensive positions, and the Normans turned back to fight, which led to the English defeat. The battle had lasted all day, but by evening King Harold was dead and his army, despite repeated stands, was defeated.

Conisbrough was now in the hands of the latest invader to our shores.

The Harrying of the North

We always look at the Norman Invasion as the last invasion on British soil, and William took exceptional measures to ensure that he kept control of his new territories to make it so.

While he was still celebrating his victory in 1067 there had been many revolts through the country and a major rebellion at the end of the year. By the summer of 1068 William had to take an army to the north where a major uprising involving the earls of Mercia and Northumbria was taking place. At this time he started his campaign of building stone castles in strategic positions, including York, in order to quell resistance. One of the Norman chroniclers of the time Orderic Vitalis attributed the success of this campaign, saying "the English, in spite of their courage and love of fighting, could put up only a weak resistance"[against the stone castles].

While the Midlands were subdued by this show of strength, the north was barely affected, with the single castle at York being the only sign of William's authority there. When a new Earl of Northumbria was appointed though, the North rallied, killing the Earl and marching to York. William was forced again to send troops to stifle the uprising and afterwards had a second castle built in York. Later in the same year though, the Danish King Sweyn started another rebellion, drawing in local Viking settlers as well as former Northumbrians who had fled north to Scotland, to seize York and destroy both the new castles and William's garrison there.

William's severe solution to this outrage ensured his grip in the country completely.

Firstly he offered the Danes Danegeld if they promised to leave in the spring, and allowed them to continue to plunder the coast. He then ensured that if the Danish armies returned they could not benefit from the land as they might expect. To do this he embarked on the 'Harrying of the North'; an extreme process in which his armies would systematically burn and destroy everything that was capable of sustaining human life including barns and store-houses full of crops, and farm animals, including those slaughtered and preserved as food for the winter. By the end of the year many were beginning to starve and, in the months that followed, thousands died as a result of famine. It was said that the famine was so bad that the starving were reduced to eating cats, dogs and even one another.

The Anglo-Saxon Chronicle reports that William went to Yorkshire in 1069 and "ruined it completely". William of Jumièges, a Norman chronicler at the time, described how the king "massacred almost the whole population, from the very young to the old and grey".

Orderic Vitalis also reported on this period in his 'Ecclesiastical history':

"He cut down many in his vengeance; destroyed the lairs of others; harried the land, and burnt homes to ashes. Nowhere else had William shown such cruelty ... In his anger he commanded that all crops and herds, chattels and food of every kind should be brought together and burned to ashes with consuming fire, so that the whole region north of the Humber might be stripped of all means of sustenance. In consequence so serious a scarcity was felt in England, and so terrible a famine fell upon the humble and defenceless populace, that more than 100,000 Christian folk of both sexes, young and old, perished of hunger ".

In statistical documents that covered the northern shires, the word that occurs time and again is 'waste'. The overwhelming majority of waste though was in Yorkshire, which accounted for more than 80 per cent of the total for all of England.

Other shires had recovered by the time of the Domesday Book survey, but in Yorkshire almost two-thirds of all holdings were described as waste in 1086. In this context 'waste' doesn't necessarily mean the complete devastation of a village, but that the land values had dropped so much due to the harrying, that even 20 years on their values had decreased so much since 1066 that they weren't able to be taxed. Comparing the statistics between 1066 and 1086, Yorkshire had lost more than 80,000 oxen and 150,000 people.

"J always said your house was warmer than mine Thomas"

Looting, burning and killing were all normal practice in those times, but William's destruction of all means of sustenance in Yorkshire was extraordinary in its absolute ruthlessness. The king must have known that the human cost would be terrible, but he went ahead with it anyway.

At the start of the New Year, William pursued the native leaders of the north as far as the river Tees, where they were forced to submit. The Danes, who predictably failed to leave as promised, were reduced to a miserable diet and considerable hardship, and when their king landed in the spring of 1070 to lead them to victory, he was quickly persuaded to make terms and leave.

The English still were determined that William could be overthrown but a further English uprising in the Fens achieved nothing, and in 1075 William put down a rebellion by the earls of Hereford, Norfolk, and Northumbria. The latter, the last surviving English earl, was executed for treason and for the rest of William's reign, there were no further uprisings in northern England.

Today we would accuse William of genocide for the harrying of the North, but at the time it was seen as a battle tactic and a great success, though never before had that amount of devastation reached so many innocent lives.

Medieval Feudalism and the Domesday Book

When the Normans arrived in England in 1066 they found a kingdom which already had an established government, divided into the districts we are familiar with today, which had evolved during the Danelaw. Still working under the old feudal system, there were many areas of Common land where people could graze their animals and hunt, but on his accession William declared them all royal hunting forests or parks, protected by severe forest laws. In these laws it was illegal to hunt or trap any animals in the parks; pick up fallen branches for firewood or pick fruit or berries, so peasants would have effectively lost a large portion of their productive land and resources.

William's survey of England in 1086, now known as the Doomsday Book, recorded a land governed by the feudal system with William as its head. Every level of society was under an obligation of service to the class above, and the Domesday survey was commissioned to establish how much tax King William could take from his newly conquered land.

The basic unit of land in the Domesday survey is the manor, which could be larger or smaller than just one village, and formed part of larger areas of land, the Wapentakes.

The value of a manor was an estimate of the money its lord would receive annually from his peasants, including the annual dues paid by a mill or mine, a proportion of the eels caught or pigs kept, etc.

The figures in the Domesday entries giving the actual number of ploughs are the best guide to the agricultural yield of the manor. A plough team consisted of eight oxen and either belonged to the lord who had peasants working them for him or belonged to the peasants themselves.

According to the Domesday Book, The Manor of Conisbrough with tenant in chief William de Warenne, included lands in 28 villages and townships scattered throughout South Yorkshire, including Anston, Aston, Aughton, Barnburgh, Bilham, Braithwell, Bramley, Bramwith, Clifton, Cusworth, Dalton, Dinnington, Edenthorpe, Fishlake, Greasbrough, Harthill, Hatfield, Hoyland, Kirk Sandall, Long Sandall, Ravenfield, Stainforth, Thorne, Tudworth, Wales, Whiston and Wilsick.

Conisbrough itself had a recorded population of 33 households in 1086, putting it in the largest 40% of settlements recorded in Domesday. Of the 33 households 21 were villagers; 11 smallholders and 1 was a priest. The village had 59 ploughlands, with 5 plough teams belonging to the lord and 11 owned by tenants.

It also had 1 league of woodland; the church and two mills, value 1 pound 12 shillings. Local historians believe that these mills could have been the old mill at Castle Mill (previously Castle Inn) and the Corn Mill on the Don at Burcroft, but there is no direct evidence of this, and though both are very old, remains of other mills are also to be found along the brook running down to the river. Inhabitants of the valley had been altering the watercourses for their own purposes since these early times; with weirs and dams constructed to harness the flow and supply the water mills which were built to grind corn for flour. Conisbrough's inhabitants were forced to grind their corn at the Lord's mill which was often a bone of contention as he could charge what he wanted for the 'privilege'.

It may have been at this time that the ponds at Mill Piece were created by damming the brook to create fishing ponds to serve the lord while he was visiting, but they also meant employment for local peasants. The dammed brook would also have created a good head of water for the Castle Mill.

The manorial system was a method of controlling territory and population. William needed to subdue future rebellion and establish his authority in a system where laws could be enforced. The system relied on the premise that all the conquered land belonged to the king. William gifted parcels of his newly conquered land to his most important followers, in reward for their assistance in the Norman Conquest over the course of the next few years. The individual estates were often scattered throughout the country; when William de Warenne gained Conisbrough and its fee, he was also gifted large estates in Norfolk and Sussex.

The lord's role was to oversee the manorial lands as if they were his own. Manorial courts were set up in which the lord or his representative settled disputes and legal matters within the manor.

William did little to change the administration of the country though the old institutions and practices had to be changed in response to the problems of ruling a conquered land. The Anglo-Saxon council became the 'Cura Regis' or King's Court. This was held three times a year at Christmas; Easter and Whitsun then his barons and earls dealt with disputes and signed treaties- much as King Ethelred had done in his time.

William did well from the financial system that he had inherited and even brought back taxing similar to the Danegeld which Edward the Confessor had dropped. He had generous revenues from his estates and a cut of all the fines raised at judicial courts. Justice in the form of fines was a valuable business in the Middle Ages. Domesday records that while the yields of a hundred or wapentake went to the holder of the manor, money raised through the courts in fines were divided by the earl and king, with the king receiving two thirds from the justice system of the manor.

As mentioned previously, the system of landholding was based on the rigid social hierarchy of the feudal system, so than rather being owned, land was held from a member of society higher up the social tree culminating with the king.

The Church rulers and barons were next in line to the king, with the barons holding their land in return for the promise of military service. They had to provide a specified number of knights for the king, which were initially taken directly from the lord's own household. Eventually the lords would give some of their own lands to knights with the understanding that they would serve the lord in the same way as they in turn served the king. It was understood these military units were only to be used by the lords for the king's purposes, and not for private warfare. More fighting forces were secured by the king in the form of mercenaries who he set up in the numerous stone castles which were being constructed. These ensured that any potential uprisings would be nipped in the bud.

After the barons and lords came the under-tenant, or sokeman, who held his land by attending the court of his lord and by paying him rent or providing a service. And so it continued, with villagers and peasants who earned their opportunity to hold a small amount of land, by working on the lord's land for a set number of days per week, and paying rent, and slaves, who held no land of their own. Slavery had been around since Roman times and was not viewed in the same way as it is today. With very little social or geographical mobility for the lowest tier of society, slaves would have lived along the same lines as free peasants but be owned by the local landholder, and their whole life was dictated by their local landlord including who they could marry.

The First William de Warenne

William de Warenne is first mentioned after the battle of Mortemer in 1054 when he was given Mortemer and Bellencombre Castles and lands fighting for Duke William of Normandy, soon to be known as William the Conqueror. Even though he was probably only around nineteen, he proved himself in battle and soon became one of William the Conqueror's favourites. He was part of the Council at Lillebonne, where William the Conqueror planned the invasion of England with his most trusted followers, and was with him at the battle of Hastings. He was amply rewarded for his loyalty, receiving around three hundred manors throughout England over the next few years, with his main estates being Lewes in Sussex, Castle Acre in Norfolk and Conisbrough. Though this spread of lands may seem impractical, especially as travel was so difficult in those days, it was a tactic used by William the Conqueror to avoid his barons holding large swathes of adjoining land and potentially staging a power struggle with the crown.

The first manor bestowed on William was Lewes, where he built a motte and bailey castle complex, unusually with two mottes. The only other castle in England to have the same format is Lincoln Castle. The first motte, known as Brack Mount, was completed soon after the Norman Conquest and the second, known as the Keep, was completed a bit later.

William married Gundrada sometime around 1070. She was a Flemish noblewoman with connections to William the Conqueror's wife, Queen Matilda. It was Gundrada who inherited the village of Acre (now Castle Acre) in 1070. The estate had been given to her family after the conquest and became central to William's East Anglian lands, being the couple's main residence. The castle, like the ones in Lewes and Conisbrough, had earthwork enclosures, but in one of the enclosures at Castle Acre, William constructed a chalk-built house for their comfort and as a status symbol.

Conisbrough was the most northerly of William's estates and was still the centre of the major former royal estate which is now in South Yorkshire. This included the deer park which had the same boundaries of the supposed Roman estate. The park boundary came close to three settlements: Clifton, to the east, Firsby to the west and Micklebring to the south. The park once extended further north, but was constricted by the development of Conisbrough village around the church. The area from Conisbrough to Clifton and beyond is still known as Conisbrough Parks in acknowledgement of this deer park.

William didn't spend much time in Conisbrough, preferring to develop his property at Castle Acre. In those days Conisbrough castle site was little more than a lookout fortification away from the main fortified burgh, built around the church; but it is thought that in around 1070 William added a wooden motte and bailey, surrounded by wooden palisades and earthworks upgrading the fort and making it more familiar to what we see today. He probably would have taken advantage of the deer park with his wealthy friends, visiting Conisbrough for recreation. Apart from this, there would not have been much change or interference in local affairs, as long as the steward he left in charge while he was away was a fair man.

Gundrada's brothers did not marry it would seem, as she inherited all of their lands in Norfolk, Suffolk and Cambridgeshire, adding to the couple's vast land portfolio over the years.

William's favour with the king continued after the invasion, so much so that when King William had to return to Normandy in 1067, he chose William de Warenne as one of the men he trusted to oversee the ruling of the country in his absence alongside William the

Conqueror's half-brother Bishop Odo. He was part of the force which quelled the rebels at the Isle of Ely in 1071. A strong Viking force and the English rebels headed by Hereward the Wake plundered the treasuries of the monasteries and abbeys and staged ambushes throughout the fens armed with javelins and catapults. The Norman forces in their heavy armour struggled to fight in the watery conditions and many were lost in the swamplands which surrounded Ely. William de Warenne was part of the conflict, trying to hunt down Hereward the Wake, who had killed his brother-in-law Frederick the year before, as the Normans finally grasped control of Ely. We will probably never know if he did succeed in killing Hereward as there are many conflicting stories of what happened to Hereward after the Battle of Ely, though many of the rebel leaders were either imprisoned or mutilated. William supported the king again in 1075 during the rebellion of the Earls in Norfolk and would continue to support him as a military commander for over twenty years, fighting both in England and abroad for him.

William and Gundrada went on pilgrimage to Rome in 1077, but due to war in Italy they only got as far as the abbey of Cluny in Burgundy, where they stayed. They were so impressed by the high standard of religious life at the abbey that on their return to England they founded the first Clunic priory in England on their estate at Lewes. All the churches on their estates were given to the priory. William brought a small community of Cluniac monks to Castle Acre from his own foundation abbey at Lewes sometime between 1081 and 1085.

Despite his commitments to the king taking up much of his time, William seems to have been a good landowner, improving the economy of most of his estates. He more than tripled his sheep flock at Castle Acre and increased the value of his Conisbrough estate in the first 20 years of his lordship at a time when the rest of the county was still recovering from the Harrying of the North and most manors were deemed 'waste' and of no taxable

value. The valuation of the village per annum to the lord in 1066 was 18 pounds which rose to 30 pounds in 1086.

William and Gundrada had 3 children together. Their eldest son, William, would succeed his father as Earl of Surrey and de Warenne. They had a second son, Reynold de Warenne, and a daughter, Edith.

Gundrada died in childbirth in 1085, and was buried in the chapter house at Lewes. William did marry again, this time to the sister of Richard Guet, a landowner from Normandy, though her name has been lost in time.

On William the Conqueror's death in 1088 William Rufus, the king's second son, was crowned King of England. William's eldest son, Robert Curthose, had inherited the dukedom of Normandy, but he soon set his sights on ruling England too. Bishop Odo who had been William the Conqueror's right hand man at the beginning of his reign, but whose greed for riches and power had ended with him being imprisoned for the last part of the king's reign, joined the plot to overthrow Rufus and replace him with Robert. The rebellion failed and Odo was stripped of all of his ranks in England and banished to Normandy. William de Warenne had supported the new King throughout this rebellion, and in recognition he was created Earl of Surrey in 1088. He enjoyed his new title only for a short time, having been badly wounded at the siege of Pevensey Castle during the rebellion. He succumbed to his wounds and died in June the same year and was buried near Gundrada in the chapter house at Lewes.

A few days after her husband's death, William's second wife attempted to gift 100 shillings to Ely Abbey in restitution for damage caused by her husband during the rebellion there, but the monks refused the donation, preferring that William de Warenne's departing soul be claimed by demons.

William's estates, along with his wife's, acquired over the course of the reign of William the Conqueror and his son, had elevated him to one of the wealthiest and most influential people of his time.

William Rufus, second eldest son of William the Conqueror, took the throne of England in 1087 despite attempted rebellions from the barons against him. He died in 1100 in suspicious circumstances during a hunt in the New Forest. He should have been succeeded by his older brother Robert Curthose, but Robert was away on Crusade and his younger brother Henry took the crown.

The Dynasty continues

William de Warenne, second Earl of Surrey, had succeeded his father in 1088 but, unlike his father, William sided with Henry's older brother in his attempt to claim his place as king after returning from the Crusades. But the English supported Henry, Duke Robert was defeated and William de Warenne was disinherited by Henry for his part in the coup and returned to Normandy. Henry I eventually pardoned de Warenne and he was restored to favour in 1103. In 1106 William distinguished himself at the battle of Tenchebrai during Henry I's conquest of Normandy against Curthose, and again at the Battle of Bremule in 1119 when he helped Henry defend his lands in Normandy against the French king Louis VI. He became one of the king's closest friends and councillors, remaining loyal for the rest of his life and was one of the earls present at Henry I's death in December 1135 at Lyons-la-Foret.

In 1106, probably due to his part in the battle of Tenchebrai, Henry I added to William's Yorkshire estates with a gift of the extensive and valuable manor of Wakefield. In 1086, after the Harrying of the North, Wakefield Manor and its farmlands had decreased in value from £60 to only £15 and nearly all the villages were described as 'waste'. As well as being an estate where William de Warenne could make his mark and raise the estate to its former glory, it was strategically important; being well placed to guard the entrance into Yorkshire via Calderdale and, along with Conisbrough, provide support in controlling north-south routes into and out of the county.

William established this secondary Yorkshire seat at Sandal Castle. The castle may have been on the site of an earlier fortification and was an earthwork motte and bailey with timber fortifications, probably completed in 1130. The castle was one of two originally built to defend a crossing point of the River Calder at Wakefield; the other castle, on Lowe Hill, was an old earthwork dating back to Anglo-Saxon times.

There is little documentary evidence for the history of Conisbrough or its castle around this time, but we do know that in 1121 the second earl renewed the pledge to give the living and income from the church at Conisbrough to his father's priory at Lewes together with the Churches at Braithwell, Dinnington, Harthill, Fishlake and Hatfield and the Chapels of Thorne and Armthorpe. In turn, Lewes Priory was to pay a fixed sum of 50s a year to the abbey at Cluny, and Cluny had the sole right of appointing the prior and admitting new monks to their English priory.

William de Warenne had looked to marry Matilda of Scotland in 1093 but she went on to marry Henry I, so he looked elsewhere for a bride. Eventually he set his sights on Isabel de Vermandois, the granddaughter of the King of France. Isabel was already married to a man 35 years her senior in a marriage arranged by her father when she was 11. This did not seem to deter the earl, and it was rumoured that the pair carried on an affair while Isabel tried to get a divorce from her husband Robert de Beaumont, Count of Meulan. The chronicler Henry of Huntingdon had de Warenne attempting to kidnap Isabel and her husband dying of shame following his wife's betrayal. Whatever the truth of the matter was, after the count's death in 1118 William and Isabel married in haste, with their son and heir, William, the future 3rd earl being born in 1119. They had a second son, Reginald and a daughter Ada and, perhaps as a symbol of his love, William took the Vermandois coat of arms, the blue and yellow checks, which have become known as the 'Warenne chequer'.
William died in 1138 and was buried at his father's feet at Lewes Priory. Isabel survived him, dying around 1147. She was also buried at Lewes Priory, close to her husband.

The Crusading Earl

Henry I's only legitimate son, William, had died in 1120 in the sinking of the White Ship on a crossing from Normandy. Henry chose to be succeeded by his daughter Matilda, Countess of Anjou, but on his death his plan was rejected by the English nobility and his nephew, Stephen of Blois was appointed as king. King Stephen was crowned in 1135 but before long the country descended into chaos and civil war.

William de Warenne third Earl of Surrey was only seventeen in 1137 when we find him serving with King Stephen in Normandy. The king had sailed there to confront Geoffrey Plantagenet, Count of Anjou who was attacking the southern boundaries of Normandy. His first experience of military conflict didn't go well, and he fled the battle along with others whom chronicler Oderic Vitalis described as "hot headed youths". A year later William accompanied his half-brother Waleran de Beaumont, from his mother's first marriage, to Paris to help produce a treaty between the English and French kings. This is the same year in which he inherited his father's estates and took over his responsibilities. William married Adela de Talvas, known as Ela, daughter of Count William III of Ponthieu. They would only have one child, a daughter, called Isabel.

In February 1141 William was with his half-brother again supporting King Stephen at the Battle of Lincoln but again fled at the initial charge of the enemy forces. This first Battle of Lincoln was the start of the long running power struggle between King Stephen and Empress Matilda known as the 'Anarchy'. Stephen was captured during the battle, imprisoned, and deposed while Matilda ruled for a short time. William and Waleran both joined Queen Matilda's side, but on King Stephen's release after the siege of Winchester the same year, they were once again named amongst the king's followers.

This erratic behaviour by William may be explained by a description of him by the chronicler Henry of Huntingdon, writing at the time, who describes him as "... a manifest adulterer and distinguished lecher, a faithful follower of Bacchus, though unacquainted with Mars, smelling of wine, unaccustomed of warfare...." he allegedly also 'stole' the Count of Aumale's wife.

The Battle of Lincoln was not the end of the conflict, and the civil war dragged on with neither side gaining an advantage for many more years. While Stephen controlled much of the south east and Matilda the south west, the barons in East Anglia and the north of the country tussled for power with widespread devastation in many regions. It was probably at this time of turmoil that the third Earl started to build an earthwork motte and two-bailey structure at Wakefield. The earliest record of Wakefield Castle (on Lowe Hill) is from 1170 in a list of constables of the area. There are suggestions that the basis of the hill may have been built in Roman or Danish times.

At Castle Acre he heightened the castle's earth ramparts, topped them with a stone wall, and began to convert the stone house into a defensible 'great tower'. It was probably he too who re-planned the town, surrounding it with massive earth banks and deep ditches.

Although the conflict between Stephen and Matilda was still not resolved in 1146, Earl Warenne and Waleran took crusading vows at the Council of Vézelay. They joined the army of the Second Crusade the next year, as part of King Louis VII's elite bodyguard. Although William could well afford to join the crusade, crusading was very expensive and soldiers often had to borrow money to equip themselves. Many were lured by promises of plunder and riches if they were victorious during the crusades. I imagine that to William it was seen as a grand adventure with all his laddish mates.

The Crusades were a series of wars running all through the Middle Ages starting from 1095 when the Christians of Europe tried to retake control of Jerusalem and the Holy Land from the Muslims. Jerusalem was important to a number of religions during the Middle Ages. The Jewish people revered it as the site of the original temple to God built by King Solomon; the Muslims because it is where Muhammad ascended to heaven, and to Christians, as where Christ was crucified and rose again. Soldiers on crusade were made up of high ranking knights, heavy cavalry, infantry and ranged troops such as archers or crossbowmen including peasants, and other commoners.

William would have called on his tenants in Conisbrough to fight with him, firstly in his troops defending the king in the Anarchy and then in the crusade, as part of their obligation to him. Ever since Anglo-Saxon times, men had had to be a part of their local defence force, the fyrd. All able-bodied men between the ages of 15 and 60 in all of William's estates had to equip themselves with armour and weapons according to their means and be able to serve their lord for around 60 days each year. The poorest tenants had to provide scythes and knives, richer ones bows and arrows, pikes, halberds, swords and helmets, and his

richest tenants a horse and armour. Military service was performed as their country and lord needed them, and the forces were also used to quell riots and catch criminals.

For larger conflicts like the crusades they would mostly be foot soldiers and used for minor defensive and supporting positions rather than in any leading offensive roles.

The Second Crusade in 1146, had started when the city of Edessa was conquered by the Turks and the entire population killed or sold into slavery. At the beginning of 1148 William found himself and his men marching across southwest Turkey. They fought an unsuccessful battle on the border between the Byzantine Empire and the Sultanate of Rum. Then they battled again in the area of Mount Cadmus. The Christian army was passing through Asia Minor and climbing through a mountain pass when the main body of the army went ahead too fast leaving the rear-guard of the army, with the Earl, separated from the rest. The Turks ambushed this rear-guard but despite the Royal Escort standing their ground most of the knights were killed, including William, and King Louis barely escaped with his life. De Warenne was the first name on the list of the dead in the skirmish.

Earl William's death would have been exalted in the eyes of his family and friends with the promise of eternal life and a direct entry to Paradise for Crusaders who died in the cause. In the 12th century when a person died away from home there was a custom to bury the body at the scene but remove the victim's heart, seal it up in lead and have it taken home for burial. If the heart wasn't available to the bereaved, a stone dedicated to the dead person may have been commissioned. People may that William's heart was brought back and buried at Lewes, but victims of the ambush in the mountains were not recovered.

As the third Earl died on crusade and the fourth Earl on Campaign at Toulouse, both are assumed to have been buried where they fell. Curiously, a circular lead cist containing viscera was found near the remains of William and Gundrada when their graves were moved in 1845, which may have been attributed to either Earl. But, in St Peter's Church there is an elaborately carved cenotaph in the Romanesque style, dating from around 1150-60. On the top are mounted knights, winged beasts and signs of the zodiac. On the side is a knight fighting a dragon, with a bishop holding a crozier looking on. It looks very much like the legend of St George which first appeared in this country in 1150 when it was brought back from Turkey by Crusader knights. If it is, it could be the earliest depiction of this legend in England.

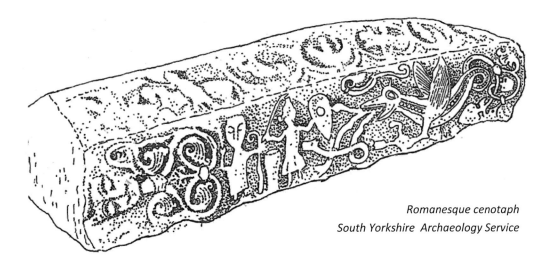

Romanesque cenotaph
South Yorkshire Archaeology Service

C H Allport writing in 1913 describes the scene on the stone with great enthusiasm:

"First of all, let me speak of the very early and curious sepulchral memorial .... It has served as the lid of a stone coffin, which must have been of a very ponderous description to bear such a weight upon it .....The sculpture is strictly Norman in all its features and diameter. The ridged lid shows two rows of interlacing roundlets running from end to end, filled with uncouth figures and beasts, not from any fixed design, but as the fancy of the sculptor chose to create them. On the front side, however, there is something of a bolder character; but the figures sprawl, and look distorted and clumsy, as all Norman figures do when they are untrammelled by supporting ornaments and above a certain stature. But there is another reason why these figures should present a wild and dismal appearance. A winged and horrible dragon ' belching forth sulphurous flame,' and with a tail that has many a sinuous fold, advances against a warrior who bears in his right hand a goodly sword, and in the left a heater-shaped shield. Behind the knight is a bishop with his right hand in the act of benediction, and holding in the left his pastoral staff..... It may be that the sculpture is intended for St. George and the Dragon....... This part of the stone may, however, merely symbolise the great struggle between the Christian, supported by the Church, and the powers of evil. It is impossible to say over whose body this stone was laid- perhaps some member of the illustrious house of Warren, which lorded it over this village and castle. At all events, the monument is of a very remarkable kind, and is well deserving of being perpetuated by the graver's art."

In his absence on crusade, the earl had still technically been in charge; his brother, Reginald de Warenne, Baron of Wormegay, managed his estates in his stead. Charters that he issued at this time had the proviso that 'if Jesus Christ brought back the earl [from the crusade] he would cause him to confirm it' or 'do his best to obtain the earl's confirmation.'

On the earl's death his estates continued to be managed by Reginald for William's wife, Ela, and his young daughter, Isabel de Warenne, who now found herself the richest heiress in England. She was swiftly married to King Stephen's youngest son, William of Blois though Reginald carried on looking after the estates for his niece and her young husband until they were of an age to take them over.

William de Warenne was only 28 years old when he died and had held the earldom for just over nine years. During his short life he had done extensive work on the family's property at Castle Acre; fortified his estate at Wakefield and had been a generous benefactor to the Church, especially the Warenne foundations at Lewes and Castle Acre.

Matilda retained the western part of England until she went back to Normandy in 1148. Her husband, Geoffrey of Anjou, had conquered Normandy in her name during 1143 while Stephen was distracted in England.

Isabel and William of Blois

In 1148 ten year old William of Blois found himself betrothed to Isabel de Warenne, as part of King Stephen's strategy to keep control the vast de Warenne lands during the Anarchy and he took on the De Warenne name. Isabel was seventeen and had probably started to take control of different aspects of the De Warenne estates alongside her uncle. William FitzRaven of Hatfield Hall near Wakefield acted as steward for the manor of Wakefield from 1148-1159 and so would have probably covered the duties of steward for Conisbrough at this time.

We'll be marrying them in nappies next!

Maybe it was Isabel who recognised that the Saxon nave wasn't big enough for the growing congregation at St Peter's Church; in any case, in 1150 the nave was widened into the north porticus and lateral chamber, supporting the walls above with three arches, two facing onto the nave, and one between the lateral chamber and porticus at right angles to the nave. Two of the rounded Norman arches are visible today on the north side of the nave. It seems that the masons utilised a Roman column topper which is on the north-west side of the church, facing you as you walk in, and though the carving was damaged in the time of Puritan iconoclasm, you can still see the figure of a Roman soldier depicted around it with his arms outstretched. It seems like one of his arms is being devoured by a serpent! The frieze along the top of this column has a wave pattern on it, thought to depict the English Channel, harking back to the crossing the Romans had taken to get here.

By 1153 the threat of a French invasion in Normandy finally forced both King Stephen and Queen Matilda to sign a peace agreement and to reach a compromise. As his part of the agreement, Stephen would remain King for the remainder of his life but Matilda's son Henry Plantagenet would succeed the throne in place of Stephen's designated heir, Eustace of Boulogne. Eustace died shortly after the treaty and King Stephen died just a year later in 1154. Henry Plantagenet succeeded to the throne as King Henry II, his accession ended the Norman dynasty and began the Angevin/Plantagenet dynasty. Henry ruled the territory from the north of England, through France and to the Pyrenees through his marriage with Eleanor of Aquitaine. On his accession to the English throne, Henry had to deal with the nobles who had built castles without the king's permission and established themselves as independent rulers during the Anarchy. Henry II immediately destroyed all the illegal castles and brought the nobles under his control, forcing them to swear fealty to him.

On his father's death William de Warenne received the lands intended for both himself and Eustace that had belonged to King Stephen before he was king. These included Mortain; Bellencombre and Mortemer in Normandy, and Pevensey, the honours of Eye and Lancaster and the castle of Norwich, making him immensely rich in his own right. Henry allowed William to retain the earldom of Surrey in right of his wife as well as his father's lands, but worried that he, or Henry's own brothers Geoffrey and William, would make a play for the throne.

 It is generally thought that William de Warenne never wavered in his support for the king, but chronicler Gervase of Canterbury, writing just after this time, tells of a plot against Henry's life in 1154 among some Flemish mercenaries. The plan was to assassinate Henry in Canterbury, and allegedly William had knowledge of this plot or was in league with the mercenaries. Whatever the truth, Henry II fled Canterbury and returned to Normandy. A year later he had a son and successor thus securing his line.

Henry knighted William in 1158 and a year later, when Henry II claimed the area around Toulouse, formally part of Aquitane but now an independent state, William de Warenne was at his side. William accompanied the king as he advanced on Toulouse but died of disease on the campaign at the age of 22 and was buried at the Poitevin abbey of Montmorel. The viscera found in a lead box near the remains of William and Gundrada at Lewes Priory probably belonged to this earl. He was succeeded as Count of Boulogne by his sister Marie.

The death of William the third earl of Surrey left a second young widow in charge of Conisbrough, this time with no successor; although married for ten years, the young couple were childless.

Hamelin and the Stone Keep

After William de Warenne's death Isabel did not remarry for several years. Henry II was determined to keep the de Warenne lands in the royal family though and planned for her to marry his younger brother, William FitzEmpress. This match was refused due to FitzEmpress being a second cousin to William of Blois. It seems that Hamelin, natural son of Geoffrey, Count of Anjou, and half-brother of Henry II was not as close a relative, and he was duly married to Isabel in 1164. Hamelin took his wife's family name, as William of Blois had done, and held the title of Earl of Surrey in her right. Whereas previous generations of the de Warenne family only visited the village as part of their annual circuit of their estates, it seems that Conisbrough became Hamelin and Isabel's favoured family residence. Evidence of this comes with the number of local charters he signed and the employment of a seneschal for Conisbrough, Ote de Tilli, to work beside him. He confirmed the grant of churches and tithe to the Priory of Lewes early on in his earldom along with the full tithe of all his eels from his Yorkshire estates

Hamelin seems to have been an avid builder and architect; presumably wanting to make a permanent mark on history in the estates he now owned. He must have spent some time in the De Warenne's lands in Normandy at the start of their marriage, as this is where he designed and built a cylindrical keep at his manor of Mortemer. Being an early style of this type of construction, he made sure that the tower was sturdy enough by adding six buttresses around it. The external masonry consisted of local knapped flint and ashlar limestone. The lower floor of the tower was a basement with no windows and entry by a trap hatch in the floor of the room above.

He would go on to construct a larger and improved version of this cylindrical keep, using all the latest techniques of castle design, right here at Conisbrough. Hamelin spent a lot of time and money on Conisbrough Castle, which took almost 10 years to complete and it rivalled any of the royal castles under construction at the time. He seems to have been a bit of a show off, incorporating all the latest innovations in his construction and I'm sure he had gained royal approval for it when Henry II, and later King John, came to visit.

Hameline's plans were bold and arty!

Roche Abbey, which had been founded in 1147, now had construction of its own, as work started on the stone church in about 1170. Mason marks show that the same masons worked on both the abbey and Conisbrough castle sites. Hamelin also built Peel Castle at Thorne. Built on the site of Peel Hill motte and bailey castle it was of a smaller, but similar, design to Conisbrough with just three large buttresses around a cylindrical tower.

Picture the scene in Conisbrough; once a quiet pastoral village, when a hoard of French masons and their retinues descended on the village and started recruiting quarry workers; stone cutters and labourers to build the largest edifice that the neighbourhood had ever seen. Massive blocks of limestone would have been cut out of the local quarries and lime kilns built to provide the mortar. In medieval times most lime kilns were temporary structures near to the site where the lime was needed; Wellgate being the site in Conisbrough. The limestone was processed in sod kilns, in which coal slack and limestone were burned in an enclosed heap covered by sods of earth to keep the temperature high. The process produced quicklime which, when mixed with sand and water, made mortar.

The influx of workers who became part of the village forced Hamelin to revisit the extension that had been made on the church just 25 years earlier. In 1175 while the castle was under construction, a fourth arch was created along the north wall of the nave and the north porticus' side wall was demolished for a new outer wall to be erected the full length of the nave to the entry porch's north western end. A squint was cut through one of the main pillars at this time to allow a view of the priest from the former lateral chamber. The chancel arch was also raised and widened and an arch added to the entrance porch. This Norman door arch with its chevron carving still survives and matches carving in the chapel of the castle keep. At this time we also catch a glimpse of the first priest, Guy Ruffus, known to hold office at St Peter's circa 1182.

The castle keep had been designed with its own chapel, and in 1189 Isabel and Hamelin created an endowment for a priest for it. The chapel was dedicated to the apostles Philip and James and the endowment of fifty shillings a year was to be paid from the mills at Conisbrough. The prayers of the officiating priest were to be for the earls of Anjou and Warenne, but especially for Earl Hamelin; Countess Isabel; King Henry II and Hamelin's father, Geoffrey, Earl of Anjou.

Life seems to have been good for the couple after the keep had been built, and they settled down to raise a family. Their eldest was a son, William, would become the sixth Earl of Surrey and alongside him were three daughters, Ela, Isabel and Matilda. Later two of Hamelin's daughters married landowners from the nearby manors of Tickhill and Sprotbrough but King John seduced one of the daughters, fathering an illegitimate child with her.

The de Warenne ties to Lewes Priory remained strong during this time with many generous endowments to the Clunic Church, but there was to be a huge rift between Hamelin and the priory in later years. It all started with the death of the prior, at which time the abbot of Cluny appointed another prior. It had been agreed from the start that the abbot would have power to appoint priors in England, though the priory was independent of the mother house in all other aspects as long as they paid the church a fee of 100 shillings a year. This agreement seems to have slipped Hamelin's mind and he objected to the prior who had been selected.

He appealed the nomination to the Pope, and, when he lost, seized the priory's possessions in Yorkshire and Norfolk. He stationed his own men to guard the gates so that messages couldn't be sent to the Pope. In Conisbrough St Peter's became one of the churches which now found itself no longer under Lewes Priory and Hamelin took their whole year's grain tithe to the castle for his own use.

The feud went on for almost five years, in which time the monks in both Lewes and Castle Acre had most of their crops and revenues withheld and had been threatened with physical violence. The Pope eventually intervened through archbishop of Canterbury and the bishops of Chichester and Ely, and it was agreed that in future when a vacancy occurred, the monks and the earl of Warenne should send representatives to Cluny. The abbot at Cluny was to nominate two suitable candidates, for the earl's representatives to choose from, and their chosen candidate would be prior. The consequences of this feud had a long lasting effect on the priory which took years to get back to its normal productive way of life.

Henry II had managed to crush a rebellion from his wife and sons, Richard and Henry, in 1173-1174 but in 1189 he was defeated by Richard who had again challenged his father in alliance with Henry's greatest rival, Philip II of France. Within just a few months of taking the throne Richard I, as he now was, left England to join the Third Crusade leaving his brother John to rule in his absence with his uncle, Hamelin, playing a prominent part in English politics while Richard was away. When Richard heard that John was trying to usurp his place on the English throne in 1192 he agreed terms with Saladin, the Muslim army's leader, and headed for home. Unfortunately he was captured and held to ransom and Hamelin was one of a number of treasurers responsible for raising 70,000 marks of silver to pay King Richard's ransom. Hamelin himself contributed £40.8.7d.

Richard ruled until 1199 when John finally was able to take the throne. Hamelin attended the coronation of his nephew King John the same year and in 1200 travelled to Lincoln to witness the King of Scotland's oath of homage.

Despite seducing Hamelin's daughter it seems that King John was forgiven as he visited Conisbrough in 1201 and was entertained at the keep. He also issued a Market Charter for the village from the Castle which allowed gatherings of more than 20 people which had been the legal limit before this time.

Conisbrough was now technically a town and an important settlement once again. It also meant that a set of gallows could be erected on Drake Head Lane and due punishment carried out.

The location of the market is unknown but it is believed that there was a village green at one time, situated at the junction of Church Street and High Street which would have been a suitable site for it.

The church c.1200, after 12th century alterations.

Possibly because of the market bringing in more townsfolk, Hamelin oversaw another extension at St Peter's around this time. He mirrored the work which had been done on the north side of the nave creating a full length aisle by knocking down the walls of the lateral chamber and porticus on the south side of the church and extending the external wall to cover the previous entrance porch door, which he turned into an archway. The new opening adjoining the nave though was very different from the rounded Norman arches of the north side, as Hamelin, with his love of all the latest trends, chose to install pointed 'perpendicular' arches with columns each with its own unique decoration. The old entrance porch was raised to form a short tower.

Hameline died in 1202 and was succeeded by his son William. Isabel died a year later aged 73, and was buried at Lewes Priory, alongside Hamelin.

The Castle Keep

Picture yourself back in medieval times visiting the castle keep for the first time. Hamelin wanted his keep to wow his visitors and show off his status and wealth, and for this he implemented as many new trends and designs as he could- his wife's vast fortune giving him carte blanche on his spend.

This keep is likely to be the tallest building you have ever seen, and the elegant sweep of the walls to the summit and the roof beyond are breathtaking. The keep tower is built of fine grained limestone blocks which almost glow above the wooden buildings and palisades surrounding it. The tower is cylindrical with a spreading base each block of which is slightly curved as well as tapered. The surfaces of the blocks are of the finest ashlar, being carefully smoothed and shaped by chisel, and very accurately joined; another marvel of the skill of the masons' work.

At the ground level the keep's diameter is 66ft slimming to 52ft from 20ft above the ground. Six buttresses are built at regular intervals around the tower projecting a further 9ft out from the tower wall and rise higher than the tower itself. The keep is entered by a door 24ft above the ground level, accessed by stone steps terminating short of the main door. The break is crossed by a drawbridge, pulled in from inside the doorway if the castle is ever under threat. When the drawbridge is pulled in, the door can be secured by massive wooden bolts pushed into the recesses on either side of the door opening. But before you enter the keep; your eye is drawn to the joggled lintel above the door- the latest in Norman fashion! (Though all the rage at the time, the joggled lintel wasn't as robust as a solid one, and the Conisbrough masons took the precaution to add an arched lintel above it for extra strength.)

At this level the tower wall is 15ft in thickness, and you walk the width of it in wonderment as you go through the vaulted passage to reach the first floor room. The only natural light in this room is from the main doorway, and if the door was closed there would be none. There is no fireplace or loophole for air and no door closing the room off from the rest of the keep. The diameter of the room is 22ft, and a circular hole in the centre of the floor opens down to a stone-vaulted basement chamber, its floor being the natural bedrock. There is a well shaft about two feet in diameter in the center of the basement floor which has been sunk sufficiently deep to ensure a constant supply of water. (Both rooms were probability used as store-rooms for provisions, and munitions in the event of a siege, but I can't help but imagine that Hamelin had a clever and elaborate pulley system constructed above this basement chamber to raise and lower provisions and water for the storeroom. A clue to this possibly comes later with Henry VIII's survey of the castle in which it states that they hadn't found the 'horse mill'. The basement floor is some 20-30ft below the ground level of the floor above and using a wooden ladder to access it with heavy loads would have been precarious. And surely if both rooms were just used for storage he would have had a door to hide it from his visitors' eyes?)

After you have marveled over Hamelin's clever pulley system you ascend to the second storey by a wide flight of steps. This winding stairway is built within the thickness of the wall, and lit by an arrow slit 31 inches wide on the inside, tapering to 4 inches wide on the outside, wider than most arrow slits from the time and probably more for show than defence. At the top of the stair is a strong door opening inwards. This room, Hamelin's state room, has a diameter of 25ft and a height of 20ft 4in. The fireplace is the first thing to catch your eye being 8ft wide, with a triple clustered pillar on either side, with carved leaves of late Romanesque and French-inspired early Gothic forms which are all the rage.

The mantelpiece is 12ft long, and is composed of several joggled stones. The chimney breast ascends in a diminishing semi-cone almost up to the ceiling, sporting a massive shield with the De Warenne chequer in pride of place.

Opposite the massive fireplace is a spacious recess, the solar, built into one of the buttresses with a south-westerly outlook, lit by a window divided into two by a heavy stone mullion. The window is decadently large, with the visitors kept away from the worst of the weather by the wooden window frames being covered in oiled vellum. Big wooden shutters stand on both sides of the window to help shut out the draughts and insulate the room. Stone ledges or seats run round the three sides of the solar, covered in cushions and rugs for informal conversations.

On the right of the entrance you will have noticed a small square recessed basin in the wall, hollowed out of solid limestone with trefoil plate tracery decoration over it and a drainage hole for ablutions. You recently heard a rumour that the only basins to be found in any other castle of this age is at King Henry II's newly built castle in Orford. The basin drains the waste water straight out to the exterior of the building! On the left of the room's entrance is a small doorway leading up some steps and along a corridor to a garderobe. Opposite the entrance to the lord's chamber is a doorway leading to another flight of stairs built into the thickness of the wall. The steps are deliberately uneven in height so as to 'wrong-foot' invaders trying to storm the castle. This staircase is lit by two arrow holes, or loopholes. The diameter of the third floor room is 27ft and the window and fireplace occupy the same relative positions as the floor below, though the fireplace is smaller than and not as ornate as the one in the room below. This is the lady's chamber and private bedchamber for Lord Hamelin and Lady Isabel. You notice that bizarrely, this room's door is bolted only from the outside on the stair leading from the main chamber but you don't like to ask why.

Nearly opposite the fireplace is a doorway leading to the family's private chapel. Built into

one of the buttresses it is 13ft long and 8ft at its widest and it is about 14ft high.

The room is beautiful, with an ornately decorated vaulted roof with the finest single dogtooth worked on one of the ribs in pride of place. This architectural motif is common in Normandy but very unusual in England at this time.

The chapel has a curious mix of French inspired decorative details along with more traditional ones such as the chevron ornamentation on the chapel's east window.

All the decoration is highlighted with bold colours and draws your eye as you enter. The chapel is rich in windows with light coming in at all times of the day. The window opposite the entrance is 6ft high, 30ins wide inside, tapering to an outside width of six inches, letting in a great deal of light which falls onto the alter underneath it. On each side is a circular light, of quatre-foil design outside, and circular inside. Below each of these side windows is a trefoil headed piscina. To the left of the entrance as you entered the chapel is a small room with at vaulted ceiling: this is a small sacristy for the priest with a loophole; another basin for the priest's personal use, and cavities for storing vestments and altar vessels.

The ramparts are reached from the bedchamber by a flight of 26 steps, narrower than the ones before. At the summit the tower walls are 12ft 6in thick. On the outside a crenelated wall, 2ft in thickness, continues to a height of 6 or 7ft as a protection for the garrison. On the inside of the rampart walk a wall, 30 inches in thickness, continues to the same height as the outside wall. This carries the conical roof which completes the building and raises the complete structure to 120ft above ground level. You explore the room underneath this roof. It is 27ft in diameter, which you guess will be occupied by the garrison once the keep is occupied. Between the two walls is the rampart walk, a safe area for the ladies to take the air. At the summit of two of the buttresses are watch-towers which can be climbed to take in the views across to the beacon at Clifton, and on to Micklebring on the first tower, and down the valley towards Mexborough castle and beyond on the other. The remaining buttress tops are used for   other purposes: The support for a wooden cantilevered covered balcony area above the chapel with a good view of the entrance door, with a storage area for wood; an oven, which could be used to heat water, sand or other material for defence, or day to day cooking, and two buttresses which contain cavities with lead cisterns, each capable of holding 650 gallons of water. In the centre of the garrison room you notice a trapdoor and you are told that there is a corresponding trapdoor on each floor of the keep from the basement chamber, which can be opened to allow for water; provisions or munitions of war to be raised by a pulley supported at the apex of the conical roof –another wonder in this amazing building!

The Annual cycle of life

There is no doubting that the life of a villein in Conisbrough wasn't easy. Their weeks consisted of working on the land and punctuated by going to church on Sunday and practising archery; and their days were restricted by the number of daylight hours in which to do their chores. Although their lives consisted of daily hard labour and barely enough food at times, it wasn't all hard work. Being guided by the Church in all things, there was scope for plenty of holy days to observe, which meant that they mostly laboured only about 260 days a year. They spent these holidays enjoying church festivals and feast days, watching wandering troupes, going to mystery plays, or dancing and making merry.

There were many saint's days but it would be the 29th June, St Peter's Day, which the people of Conisbrough would celebrate most. The day would start with a local procession followed by a large public feast. Special guilds may have been formed to organise the celebrations, with funds raised going to local charities and the maintenance of the church.

The farming cycle would begin after all the grain harvest had been brought in. The previous year's fallow fields would be ploughed and tilled ready for the new crop of winter wheat and rye which was sown in October. At this time of year pigs were allowed to pannage in the

forest, with the tenants paying a fee for the right. Winter ales were also brewed for the winter celebrations.

During the late autumn months the newly dried grain would be threshed. It was the grave's job to check the threshers' boots, pockets and shirts to make sure they weren't full of grain to take home. The term to fill your boots probably started from this custom! The grains would then have to be winnowed and sieved to remove the weed seeds and stored.

The first Christian celebration was All Saint's Day on 1st November, with priests holding vigil the night before. Although Halloween as we know it wasn't around in medieval times it was a time when people prayed for the dead and, alongside many other Christian celebrations, it coincided with the pagan tradition of Samhain when bonfires, feasting and dancing took place marking the transition from summer to winter. The dead were seen to be closer to the living at this time when only darkness, the cold and possibly death would follow until the next spring.

In November, animals were brought in from pasture. Most were slaughtered and preserved to provide meat for the winter, but the lord's livestock would be stalled in barns have had sufficient fodder and bedding put by for them to last the winter months. Their dung would be stockpiled ready to spread on the fields come the next spring. If any of the lord's animals died during the winter the grave would have to account for them and ensure their hides were removed and tanned.

Traditionally on St Martin's Day on November 12th, any final cleaning and maintenance

Was done before it became too cold to work outdoors. St Catherine's Day on November 25th was popular, as it was the traditional time for young women to perform rituals to help foretell the name of their future husband. One ritual was to peel an apple and throw the peel over your shoulder. The peel would fall into the shape of the initial of the man you were going to marry.

Advent began on the Sunday closest to St Andrew's Day on November 30th. Although it should have been a time for fasting, it was not adhered to as strictly as other fasts were, as it was seen as a time to celebrate and alleviate the hardship of the winter months. The most festive part of the season began on Christmas Eve and lasted through to Twelfth Night, the feast celebrating the arrival of the wise men to Bethlehem. Gifts would be exchanged at any time during the twelve days, but particularly on Christmas and New Year's Day and Twelfth Night. Again this celebration coincided with the pagan celebration of the lengthening of days and the Yule Log was a crucial part of the festivities, symbolically bringing light into the darkness. Homes were decorated with bay, holly, ivy, and mistletoe, and special foods marked the occasion such as pies, nuts and fruits, the boar's head, and the wassail. The people enjoyed games and dancing, and plays of a more secular nature. On the day after Christmas lords and servants might reverse roles, and those in service received a gift of a set of clothes or livery. After Twelfth Night, farmers began to plan for spring, checking their fields and doing any maintenance work needed.

At the beginning of February was Candlemas, when villagers would hold candlelit processions to herald in the start of spring. The parish priest would bless candles ready to be lit by parishioners in times of sickness. Ploughing would start at this time if the ground was thawed enough. By March lambing season had begun and the current year's fallow land ploughed for the first time. In April the previous year's winter-sown fields were ploughed and harrowed and planted with barley, peas, beans and oats.

After Shrove Tuesday when pancakes were eaten, Lent began with forty days of fasting, when no meat other than fish was to be eaten. This was the most important period in the medieval church; a time for introspection and acts of piety. On Ash Wednesday palms left over from last year's Palm Sunday were burnt and the ash used by the priest to mark each parishioner with the sign of the cross. A once yearly confession was mandatory for all Christians at this time and no marriages could take place during Lent. Easter Week began on Palm Sunday, when the villagers would bring palm leaves in the form of willow or rushes into the church to represent Christ's procession into Jerusalem. Lent finished three days before Easter Sunday and Easter Sunday was the greatest feast day of the medieval calendar, when the host (consecrated wafers of bread) and cross were carried in procession into the church, led by the great Paschal Candle, to symbolise the re-entry of light into the world. By Easter, cows were coming back into full milk, having been dried off during the winter to conserve fodder. Milk from the lord's cows was made into cheese and butter.

The weeks following Easter were good times with the fasting of Lent past, and most of the hard work of planting crops completed.

May Day was the next major celebration in festivities ranging back much further than Christian times. This was the time of fertility on what was considered to be the first day of summer when the maypoles went up for dancing and there were forays into the woods for flower gathering, and other activities no doubt! Ascension Day and Whitsunday were popular days for festivals at this time of year when the parish church sold ale to raise funds, and there would be plays, dancing and perhaps a tournament at the castle.

On Rogation Sunday the parish priest would lead his congregation in 'beating the bounds' when the parish boundaries were walked, opening up the pathways again and ensuring there were no encroachments onto the manor by neighbouring settlements. The walk was accompanied by hand bells, singing and prayers for a successful harvest; followed by a session of communal drinking.

Planting of flax and hemp for spinning would follow, with maintenance work on hedges and fences; ditches and bridges, and repairs to the roads throughout the manor. Weeding would continue all though the growing season. Harvesting and processing flax was a June activity and also the month for sheep shearing, with festivals often marking this event. Shearing produced a good income for the lord as wool was a valuable commodity. Animals were let onto the fallow fields to graze and manure them at the same time.

The Midsummer festival was the culmination of this festive season, again with echoes of pre-Christian times. Villagers would stay up all night on Midsummer's Eve burning bonfires. On Midsummer's Day there would be parades and civic processions.

After Midsummer it was time to mow the fields and prepare for haymaking, which usually happened in July. Haymaking from the lord's meadow provided the main winter fodder for the lord's livestock, which in turn ensured the land was well manured for the next year. Villagers were obliged to leave their animals on the lord's fallow land at night to achieve this.

In August, the main crops would be harvested, and all other work in rural areas would stop to get the harvest safely in. August's major feast was the Feast of the Assumption of the Virgin, which often became an early harvest festival as well. This provided a well-earned break from the heavy toil in the fields and was the time to enjoy morality and mystery plays.

In September, the last of the harvest was brought in and the celebration of 'harvest home' when the last sheaf of corn was brought into the church to mark the occasion, and seed cakes eaten. Villagers would decorate the village with boughs, singing and shouting as they went.

After the grain was threshed and the fields winnowed, came Holy Rood Day, when it was traditional to go nutting along the hedgerows. By the end of the month, the winter fields had been ploughed and sowed with rye, and by Michaelmas the harvest was over. Rents were usually due on this day, the beginning of a new agricultural year, and accounts were reckoned, as farmers now had the means to pay their debts.

It is easy to think that medieval villagers in Conisbrough may not have had any concept of time, but this annual cycle of holy days and farming seasons would have split the year up into manageable sections, with festivals and feasts to look forward to in between the constant graft of day to day living.

Conisbrough and the Magna Carta

Hamelin and Isobel's son, William de Warenne, the sixth earl, was first cousin to both King Richard I and King John. He probably grew up in Normandy, and served with King Richard in France in the 1190s. In 1204 King John lost all the English estates in Normandy including the De Warenne lands following their conquest by King Philip II of France. The lords with estates on both sides of the channel had to decide which were the most important to them and give up their others. Lords who remained in their English estates were rewarded with estates from those who had chosen to stay in Normandy. King John compensated William with lands at Grantham and Stamford in Lincolnshire. In 1206 de Warenne helped escort the king of Scotland, William the Lion, to a meeting with King John at York to ensure he would not ally himself with Philip II of France and, on a personal note, William married Maud, daughter of William Aubigny, Earl of Arundel in around 1207.

Conisbrough castle was in a 'transitional' stage at this time, with a stone keep but earthwork defences, much the same as Mortemer castle. King Philip did a lot of damage to the keep at Mortemer during this time, and afterwards it was left to decay.

Possibly because of the major destruction done to Mortemer, the sixth earl strengthened the defences of Lewes Castle, adding the South and West Towers on the keep to give archers a wider target area, and built the stone curtain walls at Conisbrough. Early stone defensive walls usually had either no projecting towers or rectangular ones, so the solid projecting circular towers of Conisbrough reflected a new advance in design believed to have been introduced by architects working for King John. Later on, round projecting towers were made large enough to be hollow to contain chambers and stairways, but this did not become common practice until the 1220s or 30s. Because solid round towers were a transitional feature in castle architecture we are able to pinpoint the moment in time when the walls at Conisbrough were erected. Records show that similar solid towers were built in King John's castles at Knaresborough and Scarborough at the same time. Thomas of Monkhill and William de Horbury were stewards of Wakefield in this period and may have overseen this building work.

King John was determined to regain his lands in France and from 1204 he spent the next ten years amassing a huge fortune by imposing levies and fines and even payments to keep in his favour, to pay for his planned invasion of France. In 1212 King John briefly entrusted the strategic castles of Bamburgh and Newcastle in Northumberland to William and made him Sheriff of Northumberland in a bid to secure his northern borders from attack.

With increasing unrest in England due to his money grabbing taxes he set sail for France in 1214 to reclaim his ancestral lands. He soon returned to England completely routed by the French and penniless. This time, when he asked for yet more money, the barons openly rebelled against him. William de Warenne played an active role negotiating with the rebels on John's behalf in an attempt to avert civil war. His efforts won out and resulted in the forming of the Magna Carta, sometimes called the first English constitution, as it set limits on the power of the Crown and set up the House of Lords to help with decision making. William is one of only four barons named in the document as standing with the King at the signing of the charter at Runnymede.

The Magna Carta outlined various laws that the barons wanted the King to enforce and obey. Much of it was focused on reforming John's present government and reducing his power but it also dealt with a wide range of other subjects including the Church, local government, the common law and the free passage of merchants overseas, among many others. It also gives us an intriguing insight of how King John and others in authority were abusing their power!

Targeting the king, the Magna Carta states that taxes should not be levied without the common consent of the newly formed assembly which comprised of 25 of his barons. He was forced to send home his foreign mercenaries; put an end to various taxes, fees and fines which he had put in place to punish his enemies, and return all hostages and lands that he had seized during this period.

The charter wasn't just concerned with the relationship between the king and barons. It included many clauses which were to rewrite the country's constitution and give people a right to appeal against injustices, though it is important to note that liberties in the Charter were granted only to free men, not to the villeins and serfs who formed the majority of the population.

The Church was protected by the charter and able to operate free from governmental interference. It acknowledged that free citizens had the right to own and inherit property; be protected from excessive taxes, and safe from illegal imprisonment or fines until their case had been heard in a court of law.

Whereas women didn't get much of a mention in the charter, it did establish that a widow would get her full allotment of lands and that she would not be forced to remarry on her husband's death. Prior to this a widow would often have to pay a large sum if she wanted to live the rest of her life unmarried. Bizarrely, the charter also absolved her of any obligation to pay her husband's debts if the debt had been with a Jewish moneylender.

It also contained provisions forbidding bribery and official misconduct by bailiffs and constables, citing that they would not be able to put anyone on trial based on just their word, take anyone's possessions, or receive money in lieu of knightly duties.

One of the fundamental changes to trade in the country was establishing a code for weights and measures, with specific measures for different commodities.

Although the Magna Carta was full of clauses around liberty and rights, it is likely that it would have made little or no difference to the lives of the peasants in Conisbrough. During the 1100s, slavery had given way to the improved status of serfs. When John came to the throne around 80 per cent of the English people were living as unfree peasants on manors holding their lands from the lord of the manor in exchange for service. Their lives were still closely regulated under the local law of the manor on which they lived, not being able to leave the manor without permission.

One clause though did address the problem serfs had with the king's forests and riverbanks. The Forest Charter restricted the amount of land that the monarchy could enclose and have control over. Nearly one third of the land of England had been designated as royal forest and access for the common people was denied. Now, there were new 'Verderers' courts, which addressed issues of trespass and poaching, imposing fines that reflected the severity of the crime, rather than offenders being maimed or killed. Thus, in Conisbrough peasants could now supplement their diet without the fear of losing their lives or limbs in the process!

In 1216 William was appointed Warden of the Cinque Ports, a vital role in the protection of England from French invasion, but before long King John rejected the Magna Carta and the First Baron's War began. This time even William de Warenne had had enough, and he sided with the rebel barons and their French allies, inviting the French Prince Louis II to take the English crown. Louis invaded and entered London unopposed. With the death of King John in 1216, one of the reasons for rebellion disappeared and William returned to the royalist side swearing fealty to the young king Henry III. The new Pope, Honorius III, supported the new king and excommunicated Louis for invading England. The fighting went on for another year, but with support from William Marshal and King John's leading French soldiers, the invaders were finally defeated in 1217, at Lincoln and in a sea battle off Sandwich. The Regency Council, headed by William Marshal, re-issued a fully revised Magna Carta in 1217 with the aim of winning back the rebels to the royalist side. William de

Warenne was rewarded with the role of Sheriff of Surrey in 1217 and became a prominent figure in the politics of Henry III's reign.

Maud had passed away in 1216, but it seems that William was not in a hurry to remarry, as it wasn't until nearly ten years later that he married Matilda Marshall, eldest daughter and co-heiress of William Marshall Earl of Pembroke and Countess of Norfolk. Marshall had acted as regent of England for the first few years of Henry III's reign so William may have met Matilda at this time. Matilda had been married to Hugh Bigod, who was one of the signatories on the first Magna Carta, but when she was left a widow in 1225 they wasted no time in tying the knot, even though she wasn't obliged to remarry given the new law.

A curious burial found in St Peter's churchyard may have hailed from this period of time. When the churchyard was cut into in 1955 for the road to be widened along Church Street, the excavations unearthed a grave cover in the boundary wall. It was only 1 meter by 50cm in size, with a sword blade carved on it, though the part of the stone that would have carried the hilt was missing. Remains found in the same area included someone who had been buried with a small shield which was about 60cm long and 50cm wide, decorated with a lion rampant which made archaeologists assume that the grave cover and remains were those of a knight. Matilda may have been accompanied by knights of her first husband, whose crest was a lion rampant, when she visited Conisbrough, or she may have been visited here by a Norfolk knight who met an untimely death and was buried in the church yard.

Whoever he was, the mystery knight is now buried in the memorial garden of the church-yard.

Matilda had had three sons from her first marriage and went on to have a daughter, Isabel, who married Hugh d'Aubigny, fifth Earl of Arundel, and a son, John, who was to become the seventh Earl de Warenne, while she was with William.

Henry III was to confirm the Magna Carta again in 1225 in order to secure taxation for new campaigns in France and William de Warenne was called on to witness it, becoming one of the few surviving earls to have witnessed both main issues of the charter.

In 1227 William had the office of Sheriff of Surrey revoked. Possibly because of this, the sixth earl joined with the king's younger brother Richard, Earl of Cornwall, in yet another baronial rebellion, but by the end of the year he had re-joined the king. Three years later, in 1230, William was made Keeper of ports on the East coast of England while the king was in Brittany, and was a member of Henry III's Council from 1237.

William died in 1240 leaving his estates to his son John.

A Tour of the Castle Bailey circa 1230

The new stone curtain walls formed one of the most important parts of the castle's defence. Not only were they an impregnable barrier to anyone wishing to attack the castle, but they also provided a vantage point for those defending the castle. The castle walls follow the line of the previous defensive wooden stockade. The timber buildings inside the bailey were rebuilt in stone too, but only the Great Hall and Chapel were bonded into the curtain wall, so the rest of the buildings may have been rebuilt after the curtain walls were completed.

Whereas the outer bailey would have housed the more industrial needs of the castle including brewing, metalworking and stabling for horses; the inner bailey was reserved for the functioning of the castle and the lord's business. It was approached over the drawbridge via the portcullised gatehouse leading to the 'S' shaped barbican and a second gatehouse with its own portcullised gate. Facing you at this point was a huge range of buildings hugging the curtain wall on the bailey's northern side.

The Great Hall was the largest of these buildings to the west of the bailey with a porch and screens passage at the eastern end, with doorways leading to the pantry and, via a pentice, to other service buildings, including a kitchen at the foot of the keep. The pantry was two storeys high, and the room above would have given access to the gallery above the screens passage for entertainments in the hall. The Great Hall was a single aisled room with a hearth in the centre and a dais at the western end.

Along the curtain wall at the west end of the bailey were accommodation suites for visiting guests with store rooms at ground level. A large chamber on the first floor in this area could have been an alternative residence for the Earl and Countess themselves, or their important guests, with a large fireplace for added luxury. In front of this range was a public latrine building emptying into a natural fissure in the ground rock. Excavations of this latrine shaft revealed tools used for working with fabric: metal sewing needles, weights for spinning thread, small scissors and a glass linen smoother. A medieval glass urinal, fragments of painted wall plaster and iron arrowheads, both for hunting and warfare, were found in the shaft too.

To the south of the bailey next to the inner gatehouse was a chapel, used each day by all the occupants of the castle for their daily religious services. Many castles of this date had their chapel next to the gatehouse so that if an enemy attacked, they would be seen to be attacking God, with all that that incurred! The top of a stone altar was discovered in this area which is now in St Peter's Church, with five consecration crosses carved into it and a niche for a relic box. Further evidence that this was the chapel comes from the discovery of a piscina under the collapsed part of the curtain wall.

At both sides of the keep are openings onto the curtain wall where a short flight of steps lead into a latrine used by the guards. The stairway continued onto the wall walk that ran around the top of the curtain wall all the way to the guardhouse. The crenelated battlements, up to 3 meters above the present wall level, would have offered very good protection for the defenders, making it almost impossible for attacking archers to hit anyone on top of the walls. In the guardhouse, next to the gate, the ground floor would have contained the guard rooms; the first floor the guard quarters and the machinery to operate the portcullis, and the top floor would be for storing weapons and siting of the murder holes.

By the Rusty Sword!

In 1239, the Conisbrough passed to John who was only eight. Matilda took custody of the castle during his minority, and the seventh Earl Warenne became a royal ward, raised at the royal court. From 1240 to late in 1241 his southern lands were in the hands of William de Munceus, constable of Lewes Castle, acting for the Crown, but the guardianship of the estates was then given to Peter of Savoy. This grant was later made to extend for 10 years from the beginning of 1242. Savoy seems to have viewed the estates as his own, as in 1242 all freemen and tenants in the late earl's Sussex lands were requested to make a donation him, in order for him to go abroad on the king's business. Some of John's inheritance was restored to him in 1248 after the death of his mother and in order for him to support his wife after his marriage to Alice de Lusignan, a half-sister to King Henry III, in 1247. The restoration of lands did not include the lands his father had held in Sussex and Surrey but John managed to retrieve the Surrey estates from Savoy in 1252 and in 1256 he was granted the third penny of the income from the county of Surrey as Earl of Surrey and soon afterwards was given full possession of the honour of Lewes and his Sussex lands.

Alice was seven years older than John and was seen as unworthy of someone of his class, her family having had humble beginnings and seen as social climbers, but the marriage seemed to be happy with three children born to the couple: Isabella, Eleanor and William. Alice tragically died in childbirth in 1256 when William was born and John never remarried.

Closer to home, William de Horbury who had been William de Warenne's steward for Wakefield, passed on his stewardship to his son Ralph in the 1250's. With civil unrest about to split the country, it would have now been his job to rally a small army for the earl to take on his campaigns and manage all the day to day affairs of his northern estates while the earl was busy at court and in the south. Tenants were still doing their land service for the lord in addition to their rent. There is mention in the court rolls of carting services owing to the mill pond at the lord's mill. The earliest surviving Court Rolls for Conisbrough date back to this earl's time and give us some insight to how the steward would have helped his lord manage the estate and fill his coffers. Unlike at the start of the medieval period, tenants now had a bit more control over how they ran their land, though the cut that the earl took both in their lifetime, in rents, court fines, licences to marry and amercements; and after their death, in heriots, was high. Although the amounts taken in fines or amercements may seem small, the amounts could be a sizeable loss to subsistence farmers.

Further work was carried out in the castle during John's ownership, including modernising the castle hall and solar in the bailey.

The Second Barons' War was looming, and was again about the power of the king and the way he exercised it. The Magna Carta had not been adhered to, as both King John and his son, Henry III, broke their promises whenever they could. The opportunity to review the charter and make the king keep his word arose in 1258, with an initial baronial reform plan known as the Provisions of Oxford, with John de Warenne backing the king, and Simon de Montfort the barons. By 1260, with no solution in sight, John switched sides against the king, obviously frustrated at the stalemate the king and parliament found themselves in, but he was back on the royalist side by 1263.

In 1264, Henry renounced the Provisions of Oxford and quarrels flared into civil war. The initial conflict reached a head when the two armies met in battle at Lewes. John de Warenne played host to King Henry III at Lewes Castle before the battle, but the battle was lost, King Henry and Prince Edward captured, and John fled to the continent where he remained for about a year with all his estates in England confiscated. His lands, with the exception of the castles of Lewes and Reigate, were now the responsibility of Gilbert de Clare, Earl of Gloucester. De Montfort became ruler of England in the name of the captive king and summoned the first directly-elected parliament in medieval Europe. However, his support began to crumble and in 1265, when Prince Edward escaped from his guards the civil war resumed. The seventh earl returned to England to fight in this new campaign, as it culminated in the Battle of Evesham, one of the bloodiest battles ever to be fought in England. De Montford's men were outnumbered three to one in the massacre, where even the nobility were not spared by being taken for ransom.

After the battle, King Henry was found unharmed and set free, and de Warenne's lands were restored to him. De Monfort's supporters continued their fight against the royalist forces until 1267 when the barons were finally defeated.

De Warenne's reward for his part in the conflict were a few more commercial properties in Southwark from which to take rents. The De Warenne's had had income from Southwark since the first earl's time from 1089 and the earl received a third part of all fees including the fairs and markets. He had a property there called Bridge House which would have been his base while at court.

The seventh earl was a spirited and violent man, used to getting his own way and not prepared to lose. He seems to have constantly tried to fence off and otherwise acquire extra lands wherever he could. One of his Yorkshire neighbours, the Lacy's of Pontefract had many disputes with him, and in the year 1268 it seems that things got out of hand in a dispute about a pasture along the earl's northern boundaries. The De Warennes and Lacy's armed their retainers and prepared for their own small war, which could have lost Earl John his Wakefield lands. Luckily the king intervened and peace was restored.

Tempers rose again in 1270 when he attended an enquiry held in the King's Court in Westminster Hall over an estate which he claimed was his. The decision went in favour of the complainants Allan, Lord Zouch, of Ashby, and his son Roger. On hearing the verdict John drew his sword and attacked them, almost killing the father and severely wounding the son. He was fined 10,000 marks, which the king later reduced to 8,400. In the aftermath of this incident he was obliged to sign a legal contract at Croydon, stating his intention to stand by the judgment of the Court after his outrage, on pain of excommunication and forfeiture of his estates.

Also in 1270 John was taken to task by Walter Giffard, Archbishop of York, for the amount he forced his Yorkshire tenants to pay him. Alexander Lucas was the steward for the manor of Wakefield in the 1270's and would have had to contend with his master's fiery temper. The earl seemed to have had full reign over his Conisbrough estates, claiming to have the right of assize of bread and beer, along with the regulation of measures; the right of judgement for hangings at Conisbrough gallows; pleas following fights which had drawn blood; namio vetito, a settlement for people whose livestock had been wrongfully impounded, and over other transgressions and claims.

When the king disputed his claim to these privileges in 1277 John de Warenne stated and that his ancestors had enjoyed them for time immemorial, except the de namio vetito, which he was willing to concede. He also claimed, as an inheritance from his ancestors, full hunting rights in the manors of Wakefield and Conisbrough and its dependencies, together with the sole right to hunt pheasant, partridge, hare, and rabbit in all his lands.

John then found himself defending his rights for his Sussex estates, when Edward I called a parliament at Gloucester in 1278, to determine which lords had usurped royal rights of legal judgement, as he sought to reclaim those lands which were due to him. John de Warenne was served a writ of Quo Warranto as a result of the proceedings, to produce proof that he was entitled to the income from his estates. Instead of producing charters to prove his right, the earl supposedly responded, in the presence of the commissioners, by drawing an old rusty sword, exclaiming that his ancestors had acquired their lands by the sword, had held them by the sword, and he would defend them by the sword. The record of the Quo Warranto proceedings shows that he was successful in maintaining his claim to the liberties of free warren, view of frankpledge, assize of bread and ale, gallows, pillory, tumbrell, thief-hanging, and wreck of the sea throughout his estate, together with his prison at Lewes.

Again in 1281 Edward I called on John to show by what right he had claimed himself a forest and all the divisions of Halifax and Holmfirth, and by what warrant he claimed gallows, assize of bread and beer, measures and rights of shedding blood and free warren on his estates. In this instance he was apparently also refusing to permit the Kings Bailiffs to enter his lands to perform their offices, except when his own bailiffs were present. At the trial John defended his rights very strenuously and apparently won his case since, by the King's Mandate afterwards: " the Archbishop of Canterbury, the Bishops of Chichester, Durham, Carlisle, Lincoln, Coventry and Lichfield were directed to offer prayers to the Throne of Grace for the health of the soul of John de Warenne and granted that all that shall perform this acceptable service, forty days of indulgence."

As we have heard, John was not a gentle master, and his officials seem to have been cut from the same cloth. During the 1280s he appointed Richard de Heydon as steward and Nigel Drury as constable for his Conisbrough estate. Archaeologists believe that the prison cell in the castle bailey wasn't excavated at the same time as the curtain walls but it seems as though it was constructed by this point in history, as de Heydon made good use of it.

From the records of the local court assizes there were tales of men and women imprisoned at Conisbrough, and of other unlawful dealings.

I will leave historian Rev J Hunter to tell us about one of them:

"What he was among his neighbours in Yorkshire, and what use was made of his stronghold at Conisbrough, we may collect from what has been told of the abbot of Roche's granger and forester at Armthorpe.

"In the neighbourhood of Armthorpe the monks of Roche Abbey possessed considerable lands, both farm and woodland; and here they established a grange with the staff of servants including a forester under the direction of a brother. Adjoining the lands belonging to the Abbey the Lord of Conisbrough possessed a good deal of land also. One day John the Forester, in the Abbot's woodland, shot an arrow at a wild doe, which struck the animal but did not prevent it making off at a good speed, followed by the forester, who eventually came up with it, dispatched it, and removed the carcase.

"Unfortunately, however, John followed the deer and slew it on the estate of the Lord of Conisbrough, and news of the trespass speedily found its way to Conisbrough Castle. Richard de Heydon, the Seneschal, at once sent off a party of his retainers under one William de Coneshal, with orders to arrest, and convey to Conisbrough Castle the good brother Richard the Granger, and John the Forester. This order was carried out and the two men were speedily lodged in the dungeon of the castle.

"One may easily conjecture the consternation of the Abbot and monks of Roche Abbey when news of this high-handed action was brought by one of the farm servants of the granger. Without loss of time, the Abbot, attended by a couple of monks, set out for Conisbrough to seek an interview with the choleric de Heydon.

"Long and acrimonious was a discussion, but nothing would appease the offended dignity of the seneschal with regard to the offence of John the Forester; he must remain his prisoner; but as to brother Richard, he would release him in consideration of the payment of a fine of £40 which the unwilling Abbot paid, and departed with the granger a sadder and a poorer man. As for the Forester, for a whole year he was kept a prisoner, and was then released, but whether as a result of the intervention of the Hundred Court is not recorded."

In the same record, the Hundred Rolls, we find Richard de Heydon, charged with having imprisoned Beatrice, the wife of William Scissor, Tailor of Rotherham, for a whole year, because she took proceedings against the earl for a tenement at Greasborough. In the inquest for this crime Richard de Heydon was charged with "devilish and innumerable oppressions".

The aforementioned Nigel Drury, Constable of the Castle and one of Heydon's men, was charged with having "come into Rotherham Town and having taken six stone of wool out of a chest belonging to a man who had been hung at Conisbrough, against the prohibition of the Bailiffs of the town" Drury was also charged with having taken a horse belonging to Roger de Bretton, together with a sackful of oats as he was on the King's Highway, and taking them to Conisbrough Castle. He claimed the goods taken were to settle a debt, a fact that was hotly disputed by the victim.

Whether Earl Warren approved of the actions of his officials is not recorded, but he probably made sure he got his share of the plunder.

Another personal tragedy befell the earl in 1286 when his only son William died following a tournament at Croydon aged only thirty. Intriguingly, the inquest to his death states that he had been ambushed and murdered after the tournament but there is no further information about his antagonist. William left a widow, Joan de Vere, and two children, John and Alice.

In 1272 Henry III died and was succeeded by his son Edward, who was away on the Ninth Crusade at the time of his father's death. John de Warenne was one of the four noblemen chosen to rule England until he returned to England in 1274 and was crowned. Edward's reign is notable for his conquest of Wales and John de Warenne, now a seasoned warrior, served in Edward I's Welsh campaigns in 1277, 1282, and 1283, receiving the Lordship of Bromfield and Yale in Wales as reward for his service.

In 1281 John's daughter Isabella married John Balliol, who had a claim to the Scottish throne. He was to gain the throne in 1292 but lost it again after the Battle of Dunbar in 1296 in which King Edward was accompanied by John de Warenne. Isabella had died shortly before her husband came to the throne so was saved from a conflict of loyalty between her father and husband. The earl was appointed "Warden of the Kingdom and Land of Scotland" and was compelled by the king to fight in the subsequent Scottish campaigns over the next few years. It seems he lived in his northern estates at this time in order to get back to Scotland if needed, but he probably resided at Bamburgh where he had been appointed constable since 1295, rather than Conisbrough.

In any event it was Bridge House, Kennington on the border of his Southwark estate where John was to die in 1304. He was interred in Lewes Priory and was succeeded by his grandson, also named John.

Conisbrough Court Rolls

The Manorial Rolls of Conisbrough are the oldest continuous record of local day to day life in England, spanning across eight centuries from 1265 to 1935. They provide us with a unique account of the working lives and relationships of Conisbrough's inhabitants.

The Manor Court was the lowest court of law in medieval England and it applied only to those who lived within the local lord's manor. Above the Manor Court was the Shire or Borough court dealing with more serious crime. Ecclesiastical courts dealt with matrimonial matters as well as cases against the clergy, and the highest court in the land was the King's Court, which met wherever the king was on his annual tour. It was a court for enforcing the King's rights, as well as acting as a supreme court of appeal, and would have been the type of court that the seventh earl would have been summoned to by the king.

The Court Rolls originated for manorial lords to keep a check on their steward's financial dealings while they were away; keeping a record of business which came before the courts and the court fees received. The range of business carried out in the Manor Court was very wide. It would deal with deaths and marriages, land tenures and disputes, petty crimes, local assizes and other feudal matters.

The lord of the manor had the right to administer justice within his manor, the most extreme of which being to execute thieves caught in possession of their thefts; but punishments were more usually of the financial kind. Access to court justice was only for freemen and above - unfree men and villeins had to turn to their local lord for private justice.

Although the Manor Court was the lord's court, and everything done in his name, it was usually presided over by his steward. In addition to the steward, there were other officers of the court:

The Bailiff was responsible for matters relating to the manor as a whole, especially freeholders. From the Conisbrough Court Rolls it is clear that the bailiff was responsible for inquisitions; the amounts owed at the Leet Courts; fealty and respite of service; for people failing to appear at court and other manorial offences.

The Constables were elected by each township in the manor to keep the peace within their area. However, this wasn't always an easy job and they would sometimes be attacked while carrying out their duties.

The Grave was an unpaid official, usually one of the more prominent tenants, who oversaw all the service works that the lord's tenants had to do for him as part of their fealty to him.

And, in disputed cases, a Jury of twelve local men, who were likely to know the people charged and their accusers. In theory this was supposed to make it helpful when deciding which of the two parties were to be believed, but could also lead to biased judgements.

Additional officers of the Court would be: Pinders, responsible for stray animals (which were secured in the pinfold); Foresters, who protected the lord's forest against encroachment and poaching; Ale tasters, who would check the quality and price of ale, and Haywards, who would maintain hedges and watch over the crops. Last but definitely not least was the scribe who had to record all of the court's transactions. Accuracy was important as previous rolls were sometimes referred to in disputed cases.

The court in Conisbrough met every three weeks throughout the year and would have gathered at the Great Hall in Conisbrough Castle's bailey. This was the Manorial Court, to which all freeholders were obliged to attend. These courts dealt with copyhold land transfers; recording deaths and marriages; managing open fields; settling disputes between individuals and manorial offences.

Additionally a twice-yearly Court Leet, or Tourn, was held after Michaelmas and Easter, to which all residents of the manor were obliged to attend. These courts included a 'view of frankpledge', at which all men over the age of twelve were bound to appear and make their 'pledge' to keep the King's Peace. So that everyone was aware of when the next Leet Court would be in a large manor like Conisbrough, the steward would summon the court by instructing manorial officers to fix a notice to the church door or have the summons read out in church.

The annual reckoning was around the Michaelmas Leet, when the bailiff and graves would have to account for rents, court profits and sales in the Manor. It also dealt with the election of bailiffs; graves; constables and of the jury for the next year. Because the graves' work was unpaid, the elected grave could get out of his obligation. In Conisbrough manor in 1319, Elias de Firsby paid 1/2 mark to the lord so that he would not have to serve the following year.

The grave himself was a villein, and was one of the more prominent copyholders, since his authority had to be accepted by his fellow villagers if he was to do his job effectively. As he himself had performed labour services on the demesne, he was familiar with what it entailed. In the Manor of Conisbrough there were three graveships: Conisbrough, Braithwell and Clifton.

The Manor Court recorded animals which had gone astray. If an animal got free it could do a lot of damage, so anyone finding a stray animal had to put it in a pinfold and report it to the pinder, who in turn would report it in the next manor court. The lord would look after the animal for up to a year and a day, by which time if the owner had not collected it, it would be claimed by the lord, or sold to the person who found the animal.

At each six monthly Leet the constables would produce a report of all the more serious transgressions. The cases could be brought to the court by constables, victims of crime, or by individuals who were in dispute over something such as debt or unpaid wages. Witnesses could be called by both sides in a disputed case, and either side could produce someone who agreed to ensure that the defendant attended court and paid whatever fine the court decided on. The constables sometimes found themselves in the line of fire while carrying out their duties, such as when St Peter's Church found itself under siege in 1325 when Constable Roger de Flete went to the church to audit the accounts of several King's Bailiffs and to impose their fees. Alan, William, John, and Elias de Vescy and others assaulted him, his men and his servants as they were conducting the audit, and they had to hide in the church for their own safety while the Vescy's besieged it! The assault must have been pretty severe as he stated that he lost his men's services for a 'great time', after the event. The same doorway is in the church today, and you can see the pockets on either side of it which would allow a wooden bar to be placed, stopping the doors from opening and providing sanctuary to the besieged constable.

While the steward or his deputy presided over the court, they did not stand in judgement. In any contested case, unless an agreement was made outside the court, an inquisition would be held, in which the jury would make a decision and then apply a penalty in accordance with the custom of the manor. It was possible for the steward to intervene if he felt the lord's interest was at stake, but this seldom happened.

Much of the time the crimes people ended up going to court over were for going 'against the assize'-selling bread, ale and meat that did not meet set regulations. The law was intended to control the quality and the measures of products produced for sale, and selling weak ale or undersized loaves of bread would be punished with an amercement, a set fine. However, as the sums collected went to the lord of the manor, the lord often had brewers, bakers and butchers amerced as a matter of course! Some examples of these infractions are: Joan le Potter who was brewing against the assize, amerced 6d; Richard Clyff constable and his fellows sworn present that the wife of Edward Wardall; the wife of William Hoseland and the wife of Richard Goodelad baked bread and sold it against the assize, so each of them is separately in amercement 2d.

"I remember when you could buy a loaf of bread, a flagon of beer and a donkey ride home for 3d."

Other crimes dealt with by the manor court were petty thefts, damage to property, letting their animals trample crops, and forest law infractions such as: Thomas Hurst because he tied up a mare in a sown field fined 4d; Person Leadbetter because he did not constrain six pigs fined 12d; Widow Lewes because she carried away a faggot of wood from the hedges fined 4d, and Arthur Burnley for a trespass in Newclose fined 4d.

Fines were especially heavy on those who committed assault and affray especially those who were found guilty of drawing blood or of going armed: Henry Leadbetter made an affray and drew blood from James Stewardson fined 3s 4d; John Hurst and Thomas Tagg were fined because they made affrays by turns and were fined 20d; the same John Hurst because he gave a box on the ear to Godfrey Roebuck, constable, in the execution of his office to keep the lord king's peace and was fined 3s 4d.

Manor courts remained a powerful force in rural England for centuries because they could be used by local communities to fulfil a large array of functions. They saw value in the courts as a community rather than something that was simply imposed on them by their feudal lords. As you can see, through the court rolls we get a tantalising taste of the day to day lives of Conisbrough villagers, and I will be dipping in to them as our local history continues to unfold.

The Last Earl De Warenne

Earl John was succeeded by his grandson, another John, in 1304. The next earl was only eighteen when his grandfather died. He had never known his father, who died when he was just six months old, closely followed by his mother when he was seven. The younger John probably lived with his grandfather until his death when he became a ward of court. He was granted seisin in April 1306, a full year before he came of age for it, and by June he was referred to as 'the present Earl of Surrey'. The same year King Edward arranged a marriage for him to ten year old Joan de Bar, the king's granddaughter, which could explain why he received his estates early. John de Donecastre is recorded as being a knight and the steward of the manor of Wakefield from 1302. He would have helped the new earl in the management of his northern estates while the couple lived in Conisbrough castle at the beginning of their married life.

It seems that from the start the marriage was not a happy one; in fact, in 1309 Edward II gave John licence "to make whom he please heir of the lands which he holds," with a hopeful addition that he could do so as long as he "will not disinherit any heir he may have by the king's [Edward II] niece". It is thought that the request for the licence was due to an illegitimate son called William, who was to be born sometime in 1310, and it may have been his imminent birth which prompted John to ask this favour of the new king. Probably due to this we find in 1313 that the earl was already separated from his young wife. In fact things had got so bad that by 1313 John was living openly with his mistress, Maud de Nerford, a noblewoman from Norfolk and possibly William's mother. Living with his mistress, and not following the Church's demands that he obeyed his marriage vows to Joan de Bar, enraged the Bishop of Chichester so much that he threatened to have the earl excommunicated. This threat became reality in 1316, but despite it the couple had two further sons, John and Thomas de Warenne. In 1316 the earl set into place a charter in which he secured Conisbrough and his other properties north of Trent for Maud and her sons on his death.

Joan de Bar was a great friend of Queen Isabella, and as such spent much of her time in London at court. She had an apartment in the Tower of London, paid for by the king. She was to often travel to France, both with the queen and on her own family's business, during the course of her life. Though no longer together, John granted Joan an allowance of two hundred pounds per annum while they pursued their divorce through the courts with a promise of lands worth 740 marks on completion of their divorce.

In 1316 it seemed at last that the divorce would be allowed, but once again judgement went against Earl John and, rightly or wrongly, he held Thomas, Earl of Lancaster, responsible for the failure of his case.

With Thomas' marriage to Alice de Lacy in October 1294, the earldoms of Lincoln and Salisbury came into his possession, followed in June 1296 by the earldoms of Lancaster, Leicester and Derby after his father's death, making him one of the most powerful barons in the country. Alice was from the neighbouring de Lacy family, one of the seventh earl's great adversaries. She, like Joan, had married when she was young, just twelve years old, and their marriage was not a happy one, with Lancaster being known as a notorious womaniser. Alice spent much of her time at Pickering Castle while her husband lived in her family's castle at Pontefract.

The earl of Lancaster had an unstable relationship with the new king, who he thought was weak, and fancied his own chances of ruling the country; he was after all grandson to Henry III. Lancaster had had a leading role in the death of the king's favourite, Piers Gaveston and the two would be on bad terms from that time on. So it could have been a plot of the king's seeking revenge for Gaveston or John de Warenne's own initiative with his feuding neighbour, which prompted what happened next...

In 1317 Alice was abducted from her manor at Canford, Dorset, by Richard de St Martin, a knight in the service of the earl of Surrey, and escorted to de Warenne's castle at Reigate. History doesn't record whether Alice went willingly, but when Lancaster retaliated by promptly divorcing her, we can imagine that she wasn't displeased with the outcome. Unfortunately Lancaster also drew together a small army of 200 men and set out to capture John de Warenne's castles of Sandal and Conisbrough, despite a writ issued by the king demanding that he should cease from doing so. On 17th November Thomas laid siege to Conisbrough Castle, gaining entry by scaling the walls after only two hours. Large sieges were important elements of medieval warfare, but some castles such as Conisbrough, were easily taken when caught by surprise and defended only by a small garrison. Once inside the castle Lancaster found only six men defending it, and while some of them, including the brothers Thomas, Henry and William Greathead, were men-at-arms, others, like an anonymous miller of Conisbrough, had no military experience. At the next Manorial Court on 6th December the Earl of Lancaster, with his constable John Lasseles, brought the six men captured to trial and found them guilty of fighting and drawing blood. They were fined 6d each.

Sandal Castle fared as badly as Conisbrough and was lost to Lancaster. According to some historians Sandal Castle was supposedly burnt to the ground, though archaeological excavation has shown no evidence for this except for a thin layer of black ash near the bottom of a barbican garderobe.

Some historians go on to say that the feud would culminate in Lancaster hunting down John and imprisoning him at Pontefract Castle. At this point Edward II intervened and an uneasy agreement was reached, under which de Warenne gave up his Yorkshire estates for his lifetime with the understanding that they would revert to the Crown or John's heirs on his death. The agreement also left Thomas of Lancaster with huge adjoining estates and a real threat to the Crown. De Warenne also acknowledged that he owed Lancaster a debt of £50,000 although none was ever collected.

In a footnote to siege; Alice later married Eubolo Lestrange with whom it was rumoured she had been having an affair with while still married to Thomas. Lestrange was killed on campaign during Second War of Scottish Independance in 1335.

Thomas wasted no time in settling into his new estates. He promptly evicted Maud de Nerford and her sons and proceeded to reap the profits of his new estates. In one warrant he authorised John de Lassell, the constable of Conisbrough, to give Nicholas de Segrave four timber trees from the wood of Conisbrough for the repairs of a building which had been burnt at Dinnington; another warrant was for the delivery of two oaks to the friars of Tickhill. There were orders for repairs to the roof of the Chapel of St Philip and St James in the castle's bailey which had been damaged in the siege, and a bill of expenses for Sir Ralph de Beeston and Sir Simon de Baldreston. These officers, employed under the earl of Lancaster, were, amongst other things, to oversee falls of wood on the de Warren estates. Baldreston had had an illustrious career under Earl Thomas, first recorded as an auditor for the earl in 1313-1314 in the honour of Leicester, and showing as being a steward for the earl along with Ralph de Beeston at Conisbrough by 1320. On 15th of September 1320 the two Stewards conducted a grand two-day feast at Conisbrough Castle, for the princely sum of 15s.4d.

The bill for the feast contained the following: "In bread bought 1s 6d; In four gallons of wine bought 2s; In twelve gallons of Ale bought at Doncaster 1s 6d; In sixteen gallons of ale bought at Conisbro 1s 4d; In Shambles, meat bought 2s; In eight Fowles bought 1s; In two geese bought 8d; In 2lbs candles bought 31/2d; In eggs bought 3d; In women's wages in fetching beer 1s; In provender for horses 1s 3d; In bread bought 8d; In one gallon of wine bought 6d; In four gallons of ale bought at Doncaster 6d; In Shambles, meat bought 8d; In two Geese bought 8d; In one fowl bought 11/2d; In ten Pidgeons bought 4d."

The two day feast is thought by some to have taken place as a celebration in connection with the completion of repairs to the bailey's chapel roof and the cost would have paid the rent for a small cottage for three years. Thomas could afford the lavish feast because with de Warenne's estates as well as his own, he was as rich as the king and had a household of over 700.

Just the next year, 1318, Lancaster was again attacking De Warenne's lands, this time in his Yale and Bromfield estates in Wales which John's grandfather had been gifted by Edward I, and again, despite appealing to the king, John was forced to surrender the lands to Lancaster. In the same year Thomas publicly pardoned everyone of all trespasses and felonies done against him, making a pointed exception of the trespasses and felonies done by the earl of Warenne!

By the autumn of 1320 John de Warenne's relationship with Maud Nerford had ended; a fact which was noted when he petitioned parliament to ask that Maud's brother be removed from a commission in Norfolk, on the grounds that "John Nerford and his commissioners were doing all the harm they could" to John, because he had "banished Maud de Nerford from his heart and ousted her from his company." It wouldn't be until 1326 though that he was able to rescind the 1316 charter in which he had bequeathed all his northern lands to Maud, though she and her sons would never have achieved them, as he outlived them.

By about 1320 it was noted that the Earl of Lancaster had completed repairs at Sandal Castle and upgraded it as a strongly defended stone fortress. But Lancaster did not hold Conisbrough or Sandal for long, as a plot by him to topple the king was revealed. He had previously sided with the Scots in their attempt at the throne, and in 1322, when he tried to prevent Edward II crossing the River Trent, all out rebellion was declared. The king issued a warrant to pursue and take Lancaster, and the earl of Warenne was only too happy to oblige. Thomas retreated back to his castle at Pontefract but eventually had to take flight towards his castle at Dunstanburgh in Northumberland. He was cut off at Boroughbridge, defeated, captured, and brought back to Pontefract where he stood trial for treason. John de Warenne's name is to be found among the peers at Thomas' trial, when Lancaster was sentenced to be hanged, drawn and quartered. The sentence was commuted to beheading due to his royal status, and he was led to a hill outside the castle, turned to face Scotland, for the pact he had made with the Scots, and beheaded.

Yale and Bromfield were restored to the eighth earl soon after Lancaster was executed, but it would take a while for him to get Conisbrough and his Yorkshire estates back as they now succeeded to the crown. Edward II granted custody of the castle of Conisbrough to Simon de Wodeham in his name.

Sir Simon de Baldreston seems to have survived the post Boroughbridge turmoil and was appointed steward of the Manor of Wakefield by Edward II after his master's rebellion.

King Edward II visited de Warenne's former northern estates in 1322 and stayed briefly at Conisbrough Castle. In 1324 he paid 40 marks for repairs to the castle walls and towers at Conisbrough and Pontefract. The gatehouse and portions of the curtain walls at Conisbrough may have been remodelled at this time, as the rough surface of the original walls are punctuated on their northwestern side by some refined ashlar masonry. He appointed William le Waller as Keeper of the Gate 'for life and during good behaviour'. William had to guard the entry to the castle and he was paid 2 pence a day as well as an allowance for his clothes. In 1324 the king committed the Yorkshire estates along with Wakefield, Sandal and Conisbrough Castles to the care of Richard Moseley. But the estate was not managed well and in 1326 the constables, porters and watchmen of the castles petitioned the king against Mosley, as he had refused to pay their wages.

In the same year John de Warenne petitioned the king for all the lands he had lost to Thomas of Lancaster saying that when he "came to Pontefract to reach a good accord [with Thomas of Lancaster] he was forced to grant these castles and lands". The king's council determined that if John could produce evidence that he had been forced to sign his estates over they would review the case. Petitioning the king at the same time though was Henry of Lancaster, brother of the late Thomas, who had had no part in the rebellion and was claiming the former de Warenne lands as his own, due to them having been confiscated from the eighth earl for the duration of his lifetime.

It looks as though the king reached a compromise when we find a warrant issued in 1327 to Henry, king's escheator, north of Trent, "not to meddle with the castles of Sandal or Coningsborough, or any of the manors of Wakefield, Thorne, Sowerby, Hatfield, and Stainford, to which the earl of Warren laid claim, they being to remain in the king's hands, to be delivered to the said Henry". If this was indeed Henry of Lancaster to which the warrant was for, it seems that he was to manage the estates, but only as the king's agent. In fact it seems that the earl of Surrey wouldn't regain his Yorkshire estates until he was one of the regents for the young Edward III after his accession in 1327. In 1331 we find Simon de Baldreston, serving as a commissioner, investigating who had entered Earl John de Warenne's chases and parks in Yorkshire, proving that John came back into his lands at Conisbrough at some point between 1327 and 1331. We also find him making grants of small portions of land in the manor of Conisbrough at this time, though it wasn't until 1334 that John finally recovered ownership of Sandal Castle from royal hands. The recovery of his estates came at a cost though, as he was ordered to pay Henry of Lancaster 2,000 marks in order to satisfy his claim. As a footnote to the siege in 1317, we find that once John de Warenne received Conisbrough back he bestowed the Market Charter on to his men at arms who had defended the castle, brothers Thomas, Henry and William Greathead. The family have kept the charter to the present day and are able to permit markets in Conisbrough and charge a fee for the privilege. In 1333 John de Warenne appointed William de Skargill forester of the chases of Wakefield and Sowerbyshire; he was to be the keeper and surveyor of vert and venison there, as well as of the earl's chases, parks and warrens in Hatfield, Thorne and Conisbrough, and of his stews and fisheries in the county of York, with daily wages of 4d.

There may have been advantages for some tenants living in Conisbrough, gained from the fact that the Earl de Warenne was the last of his line; his sons John and Thomas had both joined the crusades and by the end of 1345 they had both died. John only held a life interest in the manor, which reverted to the Crown on his death, and therefore was not as concerned about the interests of future lords of the manor. So much so that he was accused by the king of having manumitted bondmen; alienated land; and approved lands taken in from the commons in the manor.

It seems that there may have been some sort of reconciliation between Joan and John as it seems she was in his company and treated as his wife in 1327 when she travelled abroad with him on the king's business and in the years between 1331 and 1337 when various charters were signed by both parties, but she went abroad with her entire household in 1337 shortly after her brother's death and didn't return.

Suffice to say, in 1344 and 1345 the Vatican was once again directing that the earl of Surrey should be "compelled to treat with marital affections his wife". Regardless of this, in 1346 he took another mistress, Isabel de Holland, daughter of Robert Holland, a former retainer of Thomas of Lancaster. It is not proven whether John had finally secured a divorce from Joan, but Isabel was seen as his wife, as after the earl's death she is found in the Wakefield court rolls as Isabel Countess of Warren. She is described in his will as "my compaigne" which usually denotes a spouse and bequeathed her "my gold ring with the good ruby, the five gold rings placed as stars which are in my golden eagle, the complete principal vestments for my chapel, with the complete fittings for the altar, my censer of silver gilt and enamel, my golden cup with a little ewer of silver gilt, all my beds, great and small, except those which I have bequeathed to others, the great dish, the silver pot for alms, three plates for spices, all my vessels of plain silver, as in dishes, saucers, basins, washing dishes, chargers, cups and goblets, except those which I have bequeathed to others in this Testament." This seems enough proof that in John's mind at least, she was his wife. Joan was still alive in the year of the earl's death, and though she was completely ignored in his will, when she introduced a clerk to one of the Warenne's churches in Salisbury she did so under the description of "Domina Joan de Barr, Comitissa Surrey". The king stepped in again as he had done for much of Joan's life, granting her the continuation of her annual income of £200 after John's death until her passing in 1361.

In his later years the earl appears to have sought to be on better terms with the church than he had been for most of his life. He made a gift of the manor of Hatfield to the neighbouring abbey of Roche, the profits of which were enough for them to add thirteen monks to their foundation. He also founded St. Swithin's Chantry in Stanley, Wakefield. It was built for plague victims, in order for them to attend devotionals so that others could attend their parish churches without the fear of plague.

The eighth and last Earl de Warenne died on his sixty first birthday, having made his last will at Conisbrough Castle on the 24th June and passing on the 30th. On his death his northern lands went to the Crown. The Sussex lands were settled on Richard, Earl of Arundel and Surrey, John's sister's family.

Plague and Rebellion

Conisbrough reverted to the Crown on the last Earl de Warenne's death, and Edward III conferred the estate on his youngest son, Edmund Langley, who was just six years old. His mother, Queen Philippa, administered the estate for him in his minority, and was allowed to receive the profits of the estate for the education of Edmund and her other children. Edmund had been Earl John's godson so was probably familiar with Conisbrough, and he was to make the castle his secondary residence, his main one being at Fotheringhay near Peterborough.

Within a year of Edmund receiving Conisbrough though, the village would have been visited by a terrible plague which was sweeping through the country. Although there had been plagues before, the Black Death or Bubonic Plague was the second and deadliest known plague pandemic, during which England lost half of its population.

The Black Death arrived in Western European in 1347 according to the account of Michele da Piazza who wrote that in October 1347, "twelve Genoese galleys carried such a disease in their bodies that if anyone so much as spoke with one of them he was infected with the deadly illness and could not avoid death." Historians agree that sailors and merchants caught the plague in the Black Sea, and point to Central Asia as its origin. The disease was spread by rat fleas but plagues normally died back in the winter when cold weather made the fleas inactive. The plague in England seems to have started off in its bubonic strain, with the first signs being black tumours or pustules in the neck, groin or armpits sometimes growing as large as an apple. These were followed by headaches, body pain and shivering.

"Have you seen my mother Dennis?"

In the winter of 1348/49 the disease, instead of going dormant, developed into the more virulent pneumonic form, in which the infection moved to the lungs and caused the victim to cough up blood containing plague bacteria. The plague in this form went directly from one person to another and resulted in nearly 100% mortality. Having started in the south, by spring of 1349 the Black Death had reached the Midlands and continued to move north. The infections were so acute that even family members would not tend to the sick and the dying, and the dead were sometimes left to rot. Despite the image we have of bodies dumped in carts and dropped into mass graves, emergency burials of this sort were actually not that common in the middle ages and were mostly reserved for more urban areas.

There are no detailed reports of how the Black Death affected Conisbrough though it would definitely have visited the village that year. Looking through the court rolls there are seventeen descriptions of herioted land (land passed on after the owner's death) only seven of which involve the more usual descent from parent to child. Four describe the land as descending from siblings and the remaining six from kinsmen or kinswomen. The making of wills is mentioned more frequently than usual and there were at least nineteen requests by executors to administer wills, and fourteen cases of debt involving the executors of wills. Several of the executors requested administration of more than one will, such as Robert, who was the executor of Beatrice de Butterbusk, Thomas de Butterbusk and their son John, who all appeared to have died within a short space of time. Tragically the custom of bequeathing clothing and bedding to members of the family probably signed their beneficiaries' own death warrant, as fleas inhabiting the deceased's possessions transferred over to their new hosts.

Unlike the more usual reports of people breaking into the pinfold to 'rescue' their impounded animals, these rolls eerily show strays remaining unclaimed. One account shows a mare, three colts, a cow and a draught animal impounded and being left unclaimed, the profit from their sale paid into the court. Altogether, the lord profited by 15s 8d from strays during the year. These unclaimed strays along with a rise in personal conflict and violence suggests a breakdown in the normal functioning of village life, likely to have been brought on by unusually high mortality rates. It is not known whether the castle residents were affected by the plague. Most medieval chroniclers claimed that the Black Death was indiscriminate and killed people of all walks of life, age and gender. The rich though were able to cut themselves off from potentially plague carrying individuals, shutting the doors of their castles and waiting for the infections to die down. They could afford to buy cures for the plague, such as washes of sage and vinegar to apply to the pustules as soon as they appeared; sulphur for boiling in the house to fumigate it; bloodletting, and drawing the pus to reduce the buboes. They were also better nourished and therefore more able to stave off infection. Their tenants on the other hand had suffered five years of bad harvests, were malnourished and exhausted by long hours of physical work, so had little immunity to the disease. By the end of 1350 the plague had subsided, but there were further outbreaks throughout the 14th century; none, however, caused the widespread devastation of the first outbreak.

Edmund Langley didn't seem to have his older brothers' ambition or drive to add to their status and fortunes and his name appears less frequently than his brothers' in the public affairs of the reigns of Edward and Richard. He was once described as 'indolent, guileless and peaceable,' and as such may have been a popular lord for the village, being more concerned in the hunt than extorting taxes from his tenants to fund his personal feuds. The former Warenne estates formed a valuable part of Edmund's lands with two castles both fit for comfortable living; feudal rights extending over a large area and with the deer park at Conisbrough and the chase at Hatfield, providing unrivalled hunting opportunities.

It is believed that the majority of the 14th century improvements to the accommodation of the inner bailey were done during Langley's time, as the castle was more often used by him than it had been by the de Warennes. In the Great Hall the central hearth was covered over and a fireplace with a chimney built into the north wall of the hall. The curved west end of the hall had a dividing wall built across it, producing a new room into which a fireplace was built creating a snug for the lord. According to English Heritage research the hall is the only part of the castle to show any sign of a mortar render on a few of the stones on the north wall, and a similar rendering can be found on the walls of part of St Peter's Church. It is known that in 1350 the external south facing walls of the church were taken down and rebuilt in line with entry door. This was presumably done under the earl's direction, as the stone from this part of the church is of a similar quality as that found in the hall area of the castle. The church's east window is compatible with medieval work of this period and though the tracery has been replaced much of the arch is again from this time.

Edmund was created Earl of Cambridge in 1363 but he wasn't to marry until 1372 when he was 31. The king had been trying to arrange a marriage for him to Margaret of Flanders, to gain control of valuable estates in France, but when Margret married the duke of Burgundy, Edmund was married to Isabella of Castile, younger daughter of the late King Pedro 'the Cruel' of Castile. Isabella was only 17 and came to him with no lands or income, her elder sister Constanza having inherited all their father's estates, but, with his lack of ambition, Edmund was probably quite content with the arrangement. Their first son, Edward was born the following year followed by a daughter, Constance, in 1374. Isabella appears to have lived the majority of her life in England after her marriage, and was at Conisbrough for the birth of all of her children. As medieval women were confined to their chamber for several weeks before giving birth, Isabella of Castile would have spent some time at the castle.

In 1375 there was a heat wave and plague broke out again on a scale never seen before in the north. Almost the whole region was affected and among the middle classes it was said that nearly every house was deprived of its residents and left standing empty. After two major plague episodes within twenty five years there was now a drastic labour shortage on the land. Many landowners began to enclose their lands, turning to sheep farming rather than labour-intensive crop farming. With fewer labourers needed, lords often allowed villeins to purchase their freedom from their feudal obligation. Elsewhere plague survivors demanded higher wages and tenants refused to do unpaid service for feudal masters. Attempts to fix wages and prices at pre-plague rates and restrict peasants' mobility, with the Statute of Labourers bill only increased resentment.

According to Poll Tax records of 1379 the average rate of payment of the tax was 4d, and at Conisbrough the records show a potter, a swineherd, a cartwright and a franklin called de Westby paying it. By 1380 the financial demands of the Hundred Years' War, which had begun in 1337, led to the government levying three poll taxes in four years. The third tax in 1380 demanded a flat rate of 12d per adult, at which point the populace had had enough. Groups of peasants from Kent and Essex marched on London and, joined by townspeople, attacked the Government. Fourteen year old King Richard II met the rebels and agreed to their demands, but afterwards he had the leaders caught and executed, and the king's concessions were revoked.

Conflicts over wages appear in Conisbrough in this year shown in relation to unpaid wages for ploughing, mowing, harvest service and work at the mill. Some of these unpaid wages were owed by the grave of Conisbrough, William Lumbard, and may have been claimed for work on the manor or on William's own holding. In one instance the court decided that William Lumbard did owe a John Page wages for mowing, but not as much as John had claimed. Wealthier tenants could hire villeins of the manor to work on their own holdings or to perform labour services they themselves owed to the lord. This obviously lead to unscrupulous villeins getting greedy and hiring themselves out for work that they were not available for, such as the contract of service for John Rotur when three men, Elissot Neleson, William del Hill and William Thornor, all claimed to have hired him.

Landowners gradually began to lease some of their own manorial lands and common lands in an attempt to maintain their estate incomes. In Conisbrough manor, demesne leases are noted for: the castle grange, the knight's chamber, an area called 'le Shepen' and the mill, and the accounts at the end of the roll indicate some of the rents payable for lands taken in from the commons.

Possibly foreseeing potential conflict with the rebels involved in the Peasants' Revolt,

Edmund set about fortifying the castle, and the Court Rolls noted extensive repairs to the gates and the bridge at the castle with: '1 hasp of the said iron for the outer doors of the castle 3d'; '2 men cutting down 4 trees for making the gates of the glade and 1 tree for making the castle bridge 3d'; and 'Carriage of 300 planks from Wakefield to Conisbrough of the same in the year in the same castle 2d'. The deer park was still very popular with the earl it seems, as there was a report in 1392 of 550 deer killed in Conisbrough Parks.

Though seeming to be unambitious, Edmund served in the Hundred Years' War with the Black Prince in the south of France. He gained the title of the first Duke of York in Richard's reign while defending the king's interests in England against the constant threat from Henry Bolinbroke while the king was away.

There had also been trouble brewing in Portugal in 1379 over succession, when Henry of Castile died and Portugal's King John took the throne. John of Gaunt claimed the crown of Castile by right of his wife Constance, and presumably Isabella had an interest in the matter too, as Edmund formed an army to go to Portugal. Luckily tempers were quelled when the Portuguese king married his son to John of Gaunt's daughter Catherine, and Langley's army was able to return home before it left England.

In 1392 Isabella died aged 37 and was buried at Langley Priory in Hertfordshire. She had had two children with Edmund within the first two years of their marriage but it was to be another ten years before her third son was born. Whereas all of Isabella's children had been born at Conisbrough, only her third was referred to as 'of Conisbrough' a sign that he wasn't Edmund's, as illegitimate children tended to be named after the place they were born rather than the family name. Chroniclers of the time had reported that Isabella and Edmund were an ill-matched couple, citing Isabella's 'loose morals' and it seems that she may have strayed at some point, including an affair with the king's half-brother, John Holland. Another indication of the failed relationship was in Isabella's will, when she left items to all her children, her brother-in-law the duke of Lancaster and her sister-in-law the duchess of Gloucester, but nothing at all to her husband. Isabella named King Richard as her heir and asked him to grant her younger son, Richard, an annuity of 500 marks.

Almost a year after Isabella's death Edmund married Joan Holland, half-niece of Richard II. Joan brought no lands with her and was only around thirteen, some forty years younger than Edmund, and the couple were to have no children.

Langley continued to have a part in the ruling of the country. In 1394 he and John of Gaunt were in charge of talks at Leulinghen brokering Anglo-French peace. He was made Warden of the West March, the border between England and Wales; but in 1398 as keeper of England when Richard II was in Ireland, he found himself mustering a small army in an attempt to stop an invasion by Henry Bolingbroke. Finding himself pinned down at Berkeley Castle by Bolingbroke's much larger force, Edmund surrendered and switched sides against his father. Richard lost the throne as a result and Langley proved his loyalty to Bolingbroke, now Henry IV, soon afterwards, when he found out about a plot to overthrow the king. His own son Edward was implemented as part of the traitorous gang and all but one of the plotters were executed, Edward, thanks to his father, being the only one spared.

Duke Edmund died at Langley in Hertfordshire in 1402 aged 61. His elder son Edward succeeded him and became second duke of York. Although his marriage to Isabelle may have ended badly it seems he was still devoted to her, as in his will of 1400 he requested burial "near my beloved Isabele, formerly my consort." Edmund left his young widow Joan 250 marks. Joan was to marry three more times and is thought to have lived until 1434.

A walk from Firsby to Butterbusk circa 1380

We start our walk at the pottery in the little hamlet of Firsby, nestled in the valley of a tributary of Hooton Beck. The soil is heavy coal shale and clay, unsuitable for arable farming, and probably why it is part of the Conisbrough Parks. Trying to eke out a living as a farmer is a challenge, which is probably why Nicholas of Firsby, also mentioned in the Court Rolls as Nicholas the Potter, follows in his father's footsteps, digging the clay and using the coal measures from the stream bed or nearby bell pits to fire the kilns and make pottery. Though providing an important industry for villagers from near and far, being a potter is seen as being a dirty, smelly and dangerous occupation, and potters are often shunned by local people. It is hard work digging and preparing the clay, and minerals used in colouring the clay and glazes are unhealthy for the potter and anyone living nearby. The pottery made here is coarse and sand-tempered, but used widely for cooking pots, bowls, jugs, cisterns, drinking mugs, dripping dishes and curfews.

Climbing out of the valley towards Conisbrough we are in the land enclosed under Forest Law. Times have changed since Forest Law was first imposed, banning peasants completely from the Park; we can now graze livestock as part of the locals' common right, though there are still strict rules on taking timber for housing or fuel and we are not allowed to hunt game to feed our families.

We are now following the ancient path into Conisbrough which leads directly to the 700 year old St Peter's Church, gradually climbing the hillside above the Holy Well. As it is summer we can see the linen blowing in the breeze, pinned to the hillside on tenter hooks to dry and bleach. This is just part of the long process of making the fabric used to make every day practical cloth and fine linens for the rich. Each household grows enough flax for their own needs and, if possible, a little extra to sell. Flax is harvested in June and the seeds used for animal feed and linseed oil once enough has been put aside for next year's crop.

Like so many of the tasks we do, making linen is laborious and time consuming. The flax stems are soaked in water, often in purpose dug pits in a field, to rot the core. The rotting stalks smell awful and there are severe penalties for anyone allowing the waste water to seep into the waterways. Once the core has rotted the stems are dried, beaten and combed to release the fibres, to be spun and then woven. Once woven, the coarse fabric is made into bed linen, towels, head coverings and aprons. Finer linen takes more processing to bleach and soften, and this involves soaking it with lye produced from wood ashes and sometimes lime. The lye is washed out and the linen cloth stretched out in the fields to dry on tenter hooks. The process will be repeated until the preferred quality achieved, which can take anything up to sixteen weeks.

The poorer villiens literally have only the clothes on their back, but most people aren't quite that poor and usually have at least two sets of clothes, one for every day wear, and a 'Sunday best' set which is worn for church and social events. Virtually everyone is capable of sewing, and clothes are patched and mended for years. Clothes and good linen undergarments are bequeathed to heirs or donated to the poor when their owner dies. The undergarments are simple chemises or shirts which can be washed, as outer garments are not. Due to this you will notice as we carry on our walk that all manual workers wear an apron as a necessity.

More prosperous peasants and artisans have several suits of clothes made from wool or even silk depending on their status, and more than one pair of shoes, depending on their needs.

Along the valley we pass several quarries, and money can be made doing extra labouring for the lord above our regular obligation. There are many references to stone working in the Court Rolls in the 1380s: 'One and half days carriage of stone for repairing the Mill Pond'; 'Three men hired to dig the stone at various places'; 'Four workmen hired for four days carrying the stone by boat'; 'Robert Mason hired to dig 48 cartloads of stone for the work', and 'Carriage of stone from the kiln hill to the castle'. Stone working from local quarries has been a feature of Conisbrough ever since the church and castle were built.

Another way of supplementing the household income is through micro-industries. Some of these appear in the Manor Court Rolls either as licences or land rental for doing the work, or due to amercements for not abiding by the assize. Brewing is always a popular micro-industry but baking and butchering are other ways for men to supplement their income. Women can also make some money, usually by producing a surplus of their everyday chores to sell, from brewing, baking, spinning, weaving, basket making to cheese and butter making, and you can see evidence of these everyday industries as you continue into the village. Bee keeping is also a lucrative pastime if you have the aptitude, as honey and wax candles sell at a premium to the wealthy and the Church.

Talking of the Church, we are just passing St Peter's ancient church and coming to the village green where the market is held. The Market Charter has helped with the local micro-industries, as it means that Conisbrough is a gathering place for trade with nearby settlements, and excess produce and craft pieces bring in extra income for the poorer tenants. Traveling merchants and peddlars come for the market days and create extra scope for local carpenters and blacksmiths to make chests and casks for the merchants' goods and carts to transport them, and harness makers to tend to their horses' needs. Butchers, bakers, and brewers come to supply food to the market comers, and tailors and shoemakers come to supply clothing.

You see the local midwife rushing off to aid a woman in labour. Women can be paid for services as midwives, and both men and women can be paid well if they have an aptitude for healing. A few of the remedies you know about are: sage as a general 'cure all' but used mainly for any mouth and throat problems such as sore throat and ulcers; it is good for stopping bleeding and also, with other herbs, for inducing labour; Oats are useful for soothing skin conditions as a soak and as a poultice; Sulphur is boiled as a fumigation against fleas and as an inhalation for pneumonia but this is only available for the rich. Bread is used with the herb selfheal as a poultice, drawing out infection and dirt, and hemp seed is smoked to alleviate respiratory symptoms and as a relaxant for muscle spasms. Bees wax also is used by healers as a base for creams and ointments and for waxing thread for suturing wounds.

By now you are past the centre of the village and heading downhill, past the castle and towards the river. In the valley floor next to the brook are found some industries which need water for part of their process, such as the tannery and rope makers, twisting hemp and nettles for their trade. The brook has been dammed here to create a fish pond exclusively for the castle residents to have a good stock of fish on demand. It is aptly named 'Castle Dam' being in sight of the castle, and the water from it is released in a steady flow for one of the two water mills located between here and the river for grinding the tenants' corn, for a fee of course. Also at Castle Dam are the basket weavers, as there is a good wetland area to supply willow shoots and plenty of water to soak the woods used, to make them pliable enough for weaving. Hazel and oak are used for the frame of the basket and either wood, split into narrow ribbons, vines or willow shoots for the woven sides. Baskets are an everyday essential in the village, used for containing, storing and transporting items and for fishing and, although most women knew how to weave a basket, specialist basket weavers are needed for the more complex commissions.

Once at the river we can see the ferryboat waiting to take passengers over the River Don. The first record of a ferryboat here was in 1319 operated by Henry the ferryman but we think there was one here long before his time.

The ferrying rights come with a house and meadow and is another example of a by-employment alongside farming. We don't take the ferry, following the river to the east instead, and up the hill towards Doncaster along the old drove road and Drake Head Lane until we reach Butterbusk.

This is where we come on a Sunday afternoon, after the Archery Law was passed in 1252 making archery practice mandatory for all men between the ages of 15 and 60.

The lord in turn is obliged by the king to provide knights and foot soldiers for up to forty days per year. Practice is definitely needed, as archers need strong shoulder muscles to draw a bow, especially when it comes to the famous English longbows.

The most common form of archery practice is shooting at the butts. The butts at Butter-busk are man-made earth mounds, clad with turf and a rounded roof to protect the target surface from the weather. They are set up in pairs, so that they can be shot at both ways. In 1363 King Edward III ordered that "every able bodied man on feast days when he has leisure shall in his sports use bows and arrows, pellets or bolts, and shall learn and practice the art of shooting" and at the same time abolishing football "and other vain games of no value"! Even though it is an obligatory service to the lord, archery is one thing that most people do not mind doing, with competitions for distance, speed and accuracy on all event days making it a great day out!

Two Traitors and a Dowager

On Langley's death in 1402 the estates and dukedom were inherited by his elder son, Edward. Edward was already married by this time to Philippa Mohun, daughter of Lord Mohun of Dunster. She was some twenty years older than him and a widow twice over. She brought no land and had had only one son from her previous marriages, but he was to die in 1407.

An inquisition of the time shows the northern estates that Edward received from his father:
"York Writ to assign dower, 22 May 1403.
"Firstly, Conisbrough, Braithwell, and Clifton, the manors and vills, with all their members, lands and tenements, rents, services, wards, marriages, reliefs, escheats, knight's fees, advowsons, mills, suits of court of free tenants and villeins with their offspring, with hall of pleas at Conisbrough, the pond called 'Casteldame', the park of Conisbrough with game, agistment and pannage, 'housebot', 'haibot', 'feirebot' in the park, with all other profits of the offices of the bailiwick of Conisbrough, as of the offices of reeves of Conisbrough, Braithwell and Clifton.
"Then, Hatfield, the vill and lordship with a third part of the manor, two long chambers, a bakery with other small chambers adjoining, a granary in the site of the manor, with half the long stable, a third of the garden towards the north, next to the bounds there, and of a granary next to the church, that is in the east end; with the park of Hatfield with game, agistment and pannage, with 'housebot', 'haibot' and 'fairebot' in the park.'"

So Edward, Earl of Rutland, aged 26 years, became the second Duke of York, but even at this early age he had already been party to a potentially treacherous act. In 1399 he had been amongst the so-called 'Oxford Conspiracy' group who plotted an insurrection which would place the imprisoned monarch King Richard II back on the English Throne. The plot was to waylay Henry IV on his way to Oxford to attend a New Year's Royal tournament; but Edward had an uneasy conscience and had sent the new king a warning via his father. The three leading Earls in the conspiracy were caught and executed. It is uncertain how much involvement Edward had in the conspiracy, he lost his title of Duke of Albemarle but was fully acquitted by Henry IV in 1401.

Again in 1405 Edward was involved in his sister, Lady Despenser's plot to abduct the young Edmund Mortimer, Earl of March, along with his brother Roger. The plan was to put Edmund on the throne, murdering the king along the way. The boys were successfully abducted but soon recaptured. At her trial Constance successfully implicated her brother as the ringleader of the plot. As a result Edward was imprisoned in Pevensey Castle for several months, after which he was restored to the Privy Council and regained his estates.

Like many earls at the time the Duke of York was heavily in debt. He tried to use the letters of the privy seal to raise money but when that didn't work he had to promise his Yorkshire revenue to his retainers in order to keep them in his service.

His fortunes changed in 1412 when he served Henry IV in France trying to gain back Aquitaine in the Hundred Years' War. France bought them off and Edward received a £36,000 share for his part in the campaign. Henry IV died in 1413 and was succeeded by his eldest son as King Henry V.

In 1415 the Duke of York was with Henry V in his expedition to France. He led a division at Agincourt when the English won the famous victory over the French, largely thanks to the famous English longbow. It proved disastrous for the earl though, as being a very obese man, he was crushed to death amongst his own troops. Edward's widow, received a grant for life of the Lordship of the Isle of Wight, previously held by her husband.

Edward's ignominious death at Agincourt

Edward's post mortem inquisition shows some extra lands which the Duke owned and his charter is interesting for the life annuity pledged to William Canning:

"Inquisition. Doncaster. 21 Dec. 1415.
"Edward held the manor, vill and lordship of Sowerby in tail male of the king in chief by knight service by the grant of Edward III to Edmund his father annual value £53 6s.8d. Similarly he held £400 yearly from the custom of wools in the port of Kingston upon Hull and £100 from the issues of the county, part of £1,000 yearly granted by Richard II to his father when he was created duke of York. Joan widow of Edmund his father was assigned 200 marks and 50 marks from these sums in dower, and Edward held the reversion of them." By his charter of 12 Aug. 1415 he "granted to Henry bishop of Winchester and others, as above the castle and manor of Conisbrough, the manors of Braithwell, Clifton, Hatfield, Fishlake and Thorne, and the tenants have attorned to them. Hatfield is burdened with life annuities of £10 to John Horne, £6 13s 4d to Philip Beauchamp, and 26s 8d to Thomas Baker; and Conisbrough with 26s 8d to William Cannyng …Date of death as above."

Meanwhile, back in Conisbrough, by the time of Edmund's death in 1402, Edward's younger brother Richard of Conisbrough had taken up residence. Not wanting to live in Conisbrough, the Duke of York entrusted Richard to run the castle and estates on his behalf. Richard had been left nothing in his father's will; more proof that he was not Edmund's legitimate son, and although he had been promised £500 annually by Richard II, once the king was deposed by Henry IV this income was often not made, and Richard was known as 'the poorest of earls'.

Richard was knighted in 1406 and later that year, along with Lord Scrope, escorted Henry IV's daughter to Denmark for her marriage with King Eric. In 1408 Richard married Anne de Mortimer in secret with the marriage validated by the Pope later that year. It seems it was a love match, as Anne brought no lands or wealth with her, though later on the marriage did bring Richard a firm claim to the throne. They were to have a daughter and son together; Isabel and Richard but Anne died in 1411 soon after the birth of her son. She was buried at Kings Langley.

Henry V ascended the throne in 1413 and a year later Richard married Maud Clifford, the divorced wife of John Neville. Maud had successfully sued for an annulment of her first marriage and had come out of it quite well off, so she was a better marriage proposition for Richard.

Around this time too Richard was created Earl of Cambridge, his brother's former title, though it came with no lands. When Henry V ordered him to accompany him on his invasion of France in 1415 Richard struggled to raise the men and equipment needed for the campaign. Perhaps with this in mind, Richard set up a meeting at Conisbrough Castle with Lord Scrope and Sir Thomas Grey plotting to depose King Henry and place Richard's late wife Anne's brother Edmund Mortimer, the Earl of March, on the throne.

The assassination was to take place as the king left England with his three brothers just as they boarded a ship to France at Southampton. The plan was given away when Edmund Mortimer himself heard about the plot and revealed it to the king, saying he had no part in it. The three major conspirators were taken prisoner and executed for treason at Bargate in Southampton, their heads impaled on spikes for their treachery. The fleet set sail for France a few days later, along with Richard's older brother, where he would meet his fate.

Although Richard's Earl of Cambridge title was forfeited after his execution, he was not attainted, and his four year old son Richard became his heir. Within three months Edward, second Duke of York was also dead, and without an heir young Richard inherited his uncle's titles and estates too.

Richard's second wife, Maud Clifford, held Conisbrough in dower with John Wentworth of North Elmsall as her steward. She used Conisbrough Castle as her principal residence enjoying an annuity of £100 from Edmund Mortimer, perhaps given as guilt money for his part in her husband's death. She would be the last person to live mainly at Conisbrough and divided her time between here and her ancestral home of Skipton Castle. She was very close to her family and her nephew, Thomas and his family lived at Conisbrough with her for a year in 1437, while his castle was undergoing improvements.

She died on 26 August 1446 and was buried at Roche Abbey, where she had been a benefactor. She left a will in which we can enjoy a peek into how richly she lived at Conisbrough Castle, and the clothes she would have worn:
"To Thomas, Lord Clifford, my relation: a 'hall' of arras bought from Sir Robert Babthorpe; my bed of Arras with three curtains; four cushions of red silk; two long cushions of cloth.
To John Clifford, my godson: 12 silver dishes, 6 salt-cellars signed with the 'trayfulles' [trefoils] and a shell.
To Beatrice Waterton, my relation: a gold cross, which belonged to my mother; my green Primary; a diamond; my best furred robe with 'martes' [marten fur].
To Katherine Fitzwilliam: the brooch that I wear every day; a small black Primary; a jewel called Agnus Dei covered with silver and written around with pearls; my best robe furred with miniver [white stoat fur].
To Maud Clifford, my god-daughter: my best gold belt."

No mention is made in her will of her stepchildren.

Richard Duke of York

In 1416, four year old Richard was made a ward of Robert Waterton, Constable of Ponte-fract Castle, and lived with Waterton's household in Methley, near Leeds. Having inherited his uncle's title as the third Duke of York and owner of its associated estates, his wardship was much sought after, and in 1423 it was transferred to Ralph Neville, the Earl of Westmorland. Ralph Neville had twenty children who had all survived infancy, including many daughters who needed husbands. So in 1424, Neville betrothed Richard to his daughter Cecily Neville. A year later the death of his uncle Edmund Mortimer, the fifth Earl of March, bestowed on Richard another title and lands along with a valid claim to the English throne, even more superior to that of the reigning House of Lancaster. After starting life as a landless orphan of a penniless earl, he found himself at fourteen one of the richest men in England.

Richard and Cecily were married in 1429 and in 1432, when he reached his majority, Richard was given full control over his estates. The couple would go on to have seven children, the eldest being Edward, born in April 1442 in France.

Richard was active in Parliament, seen as a figure of reform and the man who could rid the government of corrupt and incompetent officials. By 1436, tax records show that the duke was at the top of the kingdom's rich list with an income of £3,230, some 50 times greater than the lowest-ranked peers.

Richard served Henry VI in France in 1436, where he funded the army himself and rose to become the king's lieutenant, commanding the whole of the army until 1446. He served a similar role in Ireland in 1447, but became frustrated that he was unable to contribute to the royal court while abroad.

He returned to England in 1450 and must have visited his Conisbrough estate, as St Peter's Church was completely remodelled at this time in the Perpendicular style, to more or less as we see it today. The chancel doubled in length and a chapel and vestry built into north side of the chancel. Later burials have made the chancel floor higher but the doorway to the vestry is still visible though it appears very short. There is a squint in the chancel which may have been used by lepers if the vestry wasn't as long as is thought, or else used by the priest to view the chancel from his vestry. The tower was built up to its full height and a spiral staircase added. The east aisle was extended to the end of the tower and an entrance porch built. The nave walls were raised at this time too and new windows installed. Earlier windows may have been reused for the north side of the church, but the windows on the side that people would enter the church from were very ornate, and surviving glass fragments include the heads of Prior Atwell and St Blaise, patron saint of the wool trade. The octagonal font is from this era too; the west face of the bowl shows Christ seated, and the east, the Resurrection. The remaining six faces have blank shields, set in quatrefoils. After this remodelling here is very little evidence of any alterations to the church for the next four hundred years.

In the rest of England dissent was rising; the king was seen as weak and his advisors incompetent. There was a peasants' rebellion in 1450 calling for the removal of corrupt court officials and a reduction in taxes. The rebels also called for Richard, Duke of York to have a prominent role in governing the country. The rebellion fizzled out but there was still unrest with rich landowners building private armies of retainers to weaken the power of the Crown at a local level. One point of unrest was between the Duke of York and Edmund Beaufort, Earl of Somerset. Richard had been replaced by Edmund at the end of the

Hundred Years' War and even with Edmund's contribution to the whole endeavour failing, he was still seen as one of the king's favourites. Edmund also laid claim to the throne through the House of Lancaster and the two men hated each other.

It all came to a head in 1453 when the Hundred Years' War ended and all England's territory in France was lost except for Calais. The king went into a mental breakdown and Richard was elected as Lord Protector of the Realm, as the senior member of the royal dynasty.

The king was ill again in 1455 and the Duke of York was again made Lord Protector. This time he used his position to imprison the Earl of Somerset in the Tower of London. Richard set about restoring law and order in the north of the country and reduced the expenditure of the royal household. But the king soon recovered and dismissed his regent, reversed all his decisions and released Somerset.

Richard and Edmund were now intent on all-out conflict to settle their differences. Richard became the leader of the Yorkist cause and the rivalry between Lancastrian and Yorkist factions would culminate in open warfare. Now known as the Wars of the Roses, the first skirmish was the Battle of St Albans in 1455 when Edmund was killed, and was the start of a struggle to rule on behalf of an unfit king, as the country fell into civil war.

In 1459, at the Battle of Ludford Bridge, the Lancastrians won and sent the Yorkists into hiding. Parliament identified Richard as a traitor, passed the death sentence on him and disinherited his heirs. He had to flee to Ireland knowing that the only way he could now keep his lands was to take the throne itself. His allies, the Neville's and Richard's son Edward, Earl of March, fled to Calais but at the beginning of 1460 they returned to England and took over London. In July they rallied for the battle of Northampton when the queen led the Lancastrian army but lost, and the king was captured. All of the Duke of York's estates had been seized, but Conisbrough still had a garrison stationed at the castle for him. In reality Conisbrough Castle played only a small part in the struggle but Edmund Fitzwilliam, from Sprotbrough, constable of the castle garrison at the time, seized a canon from Sheffield Castle after the Battle of Northampton and mounted it at Conisbrough. The Duke of York was now free to return to England and Henry VI agreed to him becoming the next king on his death. Soon afterwards though Richard claimed the throne; he lost support and the following turmoil ended in the Battle of Wakefield. Richard and his son Edmund, Earl of Rutland, were killed in the battle. Richard, Duke of York was beheaded and his head put on a spike wearing a paper crown over Micklegate Bar in York. Another son, Edward, succeeded Richard and revenged his father in 1461 at the Battle of Towton in the bloodiest battle ever fought on English soil, slaughtering the Lancastrian army. At only nineteen he was proclaimed King Edward IV.

So once again Conisbrough was a king's stronghold. The castle underwent repairs in 1482, but when Edward's brother Richard III took the throne in 1483, although the revenues from the estate would have been important for the new king, it seems he didn't have much need for the castle. John Whetley was bailiff of Conisbrough in 1485 when Henry VII came to the throne and Sir Thomas Burgh was master of the game for Hatfield, Thorne, and Conisbrough, but subsequently it was neglected and eventually become a ruin.

The Wars of the Roses were not over yet, and would re-emerge for a few more decades with Richard III eventually losing the war to the Lancastrian Henry Tudor, King Henry VII. When Henry married Elizabeth, of York, they united the two families and Parliament declared that all the estates settled on Edmund Langley should be annexed to the crown.

Later Village Life

From this time on the castle's owners lived remotely and took little interest in village affairs, other than to ensure that taxes were still coming from it. Without the spotlight being on Conisbrough the village came into a more pastoral era.

With the shortage of labourers after the plagues of the 1300s, the focus of farming is thought to have progressed from being mainly grain production to a mixed production with cattle for dairying and beef, and sheep for wool and mutton. The decline in arable farming from 1500 is reflected in in 1640 when South Yorkshire was seen as a region for stock fattening, horse breeding and dairy, reflecting the gradual change to pastureland.

During the seventeenth century a well-connected national market began to emerge in England, and farmers with larger holdings invested in improved equipment to grow crops for specific markets. They were also able to get loans and credit from their suppliers and trade over a larger area. These were the new social class of yeomen, some of whom were able to gain gentry status, using their new found wealth to climb the social ladder. They would be well educated and able to take on the local court duties as well as other community obligations, serving as graves, surveyors of the highways, churchwardens and overseeing poor relief for those who were seen as suffering through no fault of their own. The Poor Relief Act of 1662 was better known as the Settlement and Removal Act, and under it a Settlement Certificate would be issued to anyone moving from parish to parish to establish who was responsible for them should they become in need of Poor Relief. This act was to discourage vagrants accessing poor relief as a way of living if they were able to work, though it did continue to tie peasants to their parishes, especially as parishes were reluctant to issue the certificates.

Until 1555 local road maintenance had been part of the villagers' duty to his lord but by this time the feudal system was on its way out and many responsibilities were now overseen by the Parish. Tudor legislation still required every villager to provide four days of labour each year for each plough land or pasture that he owned. People who owned draught horses were expected to make a cart and two men available for the same amount of time. A surveyor of the highways was elected each year, as the grave had been in previous times, and he was tasked with ensuring that roads were well maintained and that each villager had done his allotted time on the road repair gangs. The role wasn't paid so wasn't a popular one for the up and coming Yeomen, but refusing to take it on would result in a fine. There were perks to the job though, as the serving surveyor had access to dig for gravel any-where in the parish without asking for permission, and if he had his own gravel he would be paid for its use. The free labour meant that the men of the parish needed to be organised, supervised, and a record kept of those who refused to do the work, so they could be fined. Later, the four days of labour was extended to six; a reflection of the state of the roads and also how much more activity there was on them.

The by-trades of the fifteenth century now started to become industries in their own right, though rural craftsmen would still maintain a plot of land for their own domestic needs. Basket making was one such trade, and was an important local industry in Conisbrough, using the willow plantations at Willow Vale by Kearsley Brook on Low Road.

The limestone in the area was renowned for its quality, and the quarry industry was another important local trade, with several quarries opening all along the valley, including one quaintly named as Fairy Hall Flat Quarry which was located a quarter of a mile from the River Don close to Drake Head Lane.

Copley's ironworks was mentioned at Conisbrough in 1645 and is likely to have been located on the banks of Kearsley Brook or River Don along with other water powered industries. Due to the change in agriculture to cattle rearing, Conisbrough was important in the tanning industry and even started to import skins from other areas for processing.

Flax and hemp were important plant crops in the sixteenth and seventeenth centuries. Flax was used to produce linen cloth, and canvas and hemp primarily for ropes. Demand for hemp from the Royal Navy and trading companies alike meant hemp farming in Britain was commonplace. In fact hemp was regarded as such an important commodity that during the reign of Henry VIII Acts of Parliament of 1533 and 1563 stipulated that farms of sixty or more acres had to grow a quarter acre, or rood, of hemp for every sixty acres under cultivation. In another Act of Parliament, Henry VIII made it unlawful to put any by-product of hemp or flax into rivers or streams, but only in designated pits known as retting pits. The liquid left over from soaking the stalks to soften them poisoned the fish and cattle that drank from them if they got into the watercourse. Henry's ships needed sails and ropes, but hemp was important for everyday items such as sacks, fishing and fowling nets and cloth for clothing and bedding. The growing and processing of flax and hemp could be a profitable by-industry for a peasant family and for the poorer villagers it was one of the main ways of earning a living.

The majority of villagers, however continued to eek out a living on subsistence farming, supplemented by labouring; making extra goods for local consumption, and foraging from the commons. Many farm labourers were employed under the hiring system and there was a statute fair at Conisbrough on land at the top of New Hill, below the former Eagle and Child pub, where labourers were taken on for the next season. It was common for landowners to recruit labourers from neighbouring parishes so that they could easily be sacked without the lord having to pay poor relief to them, as the Poor Relief Act would force the worker to return to his parish if he needed help.

Houses had evolved since the medieval period but were still timber framed with wattle and daub walls, though windows were larger and there would be two or three rooms even the poorest of dwellings. Roofs were usually thatched and the smoke from the fire would disperse through the roof. There were few chairs in the average house as stools, benches or chests were used instead. A sturdy table and a mattress filled with straw would complete the furniture. Rushes were strewn loose or plaited together to form a rug on the mud floors.

In wealthier houses small paned lattice windows let in more light, interior walls were heavily panelled for better insulation and heavy oak furniture became more elaborate, such as sideboards for displaying plate. Beds were no longer cloth filled with straw or leaves but feathers or woollen flock made resting more comfortable, on ornately carved four-poster beds. Chimneys were a luxury in Tudor times, and as they let the smoke from the fire out in a more efficient way, houses now started to have an extra storey for more rooms, or just one large space, the long gallery, running the length of the upper floor, used for walks, games, and displaying artwork.

Food was still cooked over open fires but baking was done in iron boxes laid on the fire or in a purpose built brick oven set into the side of the fireplace. Communal ovens would still be available for the poorer villagers. For the rich meals were both large and elaborate. Breakfast was a light snack, but the main meal of the day was dinner, which began at around eleven o'clock and lasted for three hours, with a smaller supper in the evening eating off silver, glass, or delft from Holland. The poorer villagers had bread for breakfast; dinner at noon as their only main meal of the day and would eat off wooden vessels, or pewter for the better off. Pottage or gruel would still be the staple of their diets. Both rich and poor ate bread but it varied in quality. Rich people's bread was made from fine white flour whereas poorer people ate coarse bread of barley or rye.

Practice with a longbow was still encouraged despite the advent of gunpowder and cannon. England was still proud of its archery prowess and accuracy was expected; a law of Henry VIII decreed that no one 24 years of age or older should shoot at a target less than 220 yards away. Early guns were incredibly slow to load and useless in wet weather so the Bowmen still had an important role to play in any conflict.

Conisbrough remained an agricultural village into the late eighteenth century with little industrial or commercial development. The triangular shape of the settlement with its focus on the church and castle remained, with the burgh ditch and mound slowly being levelled. Today, evidence is still around to indicate the older properties still standing in the centre of the village, most given away by being lower than the road level and also their roof lines where pantiles are bordered on their eaves by large stone tiles. By the seventeenth century the old village had its present day plan with the Moot Hall on the site of the present church hall. With the castle buildings in ruins the Moot Hall took over as the focus of the village for the Manorial Court where rents and fines were paid, land conveyance recorded and justice dispensed. Many of the Court Rolls which were produced in the Moot Hall are still in existence. The Moot Hall was demolished in 1871 when a new hall was erected and it was estimated at the time that the hall was some seven to eight hundred years old.

Just alongside the Moot Hall stood the Old Hall with its side on to Church Street. The Hall appears to be Regency at first glance from its front elevation, but on closer inspection there are clues to its earlier origins; the main door isn't quite central due to an internal load bearing wall; the roof is pantiled; it has its original stone mullion type window surrounds and there is evidence of a storm label mould running the length of the building above the first floor windows, confirming its earlier construction.

The old stone building next to the hall was a farm bailiff's cottage, it has very low wooden beams and on the outside a staircase led to the upper rooms. The family would have lived on the upper floor with animals being kept in the space below for the ultimate of comfort for the residents with free (if smelly) under floor heating!

Other stone buildings on Church Street dating back to this era are numbers 1, 7, 21 and 37. On West Street the first building on the left from Church Street is also from this era with internal stone walls three feet thick.

Slightly away from the centre of the village, The Forge is believed to be an eighteenth century structure, originally a barn, and part of a surrounding farmstead. In total there were five farms along the length of Church Street which survived from their medieval origins until virtually Victorian times. The general street plan has remained static, with the only major construction before 1787 being Low Road, which was built to improve access to Burcroft, which was becoming a centre for emerging industries.

Although the village and castle seem to have been neglected by their wealthy owners, the park at Conisbrough survived into the sixteenth century, though its hunting function seems to have been in decline. In 1481- 82 fines were still being issued for taking dry wood from it and it was noted that there were 440 fallow deer in the park as late as 1539. Hatfield Chase suffered similar neglect and by 1607 the area only had about 1000 red and fallow deer, whereas the number of deer had been described as being 'once as common as sheep upon the hills and so unruly that they ruined the country'. Hatfield Chase once famous for its fisheries and swan populations was drained in the 1600s and deforested by 1629.

In 1656 a document shows the woods around Conisbrough being leased to Thomas Bosville Pagdin Wilson. Gervais Bosville owned Conisbrough Lodge at the same time and part of the park was leased as agricultural land.

The Bosvilles (or Boswells) seem to have been an important family in Conisbrough for around two hundred years by this time. A Thomas Bosville is recorded as being born at Conisbrough Castle in 1400 (died 1460) and his son, Richard was born in 1435. Richard had two sons Edmund and Nicholas. Edmund died in 1507 and was buried in St Peter's Church. His brother Nicholas founded a chantry in the church and an arched recess was built for him when he was buried in 1521. His tomb was subsequently installed into the wall of the north aisle in 1866. Another Thomas Bosville was born in 1502 and this may be the same person who bought up land in the village in the 1520s.

Henry the Eighth and Later Years

As a result of the Harrying of the North in William the Conqueror's reign, the north of England had remained depressed and under populated for centuries. When Richard III came to the throne of England in 1483 he set about rectifying the situation. The Council of the North acted as an extension of government control and worked to improve the northern economy. The Council originally sat at Sheriff Hutton, North Yorkshire, and Sandal Castle.

Henry VIII reorganised the Council when he took power in 1509, and moved its seat to the city of York, in the building now known as King's Manor. The Council wasn't disbanded by Parliament until 1641.

In 1508 there was a survey of the lands of the Priory Manor of Lewes in Conisbrough and in 1536 when Henry VIII dissolved the monasteries he leased the Lewes Priory lands including lands at Braithwell, Dinnington, Harthill and Sandal to John Waterhouse and his son Robert for £150.5.10d per annum for 99 years.

Roche Abbey had managed to avoid Henry VIII's initial wave of destruction in his Suppression of the Monasteries in 1536, as it was one of the larger monasteries with an income of just over the £200 baseline. Over the years monastic life had been seen to flout the high standards of religious adherence and it seemed to be the smaller houses which bore the initial brunt of his dissolution, as they were monasteries that, according to the Act, "manifest sin, vicious and abominable living every day".

By 1538 though, Roche was one of the religious houses 'voluntarily' surrendering their lands, buildings and possessions. Moveable items such as furniture started to be sold, but what had begun as an orderly process degenerated into pillage, when men from the locality descended on the abandoned buildings, carrying away everything that they could.

At the Conisbrough Court of May 1538, "a prime messuage at Conisbrough called Le Hall together with 8 cottages, 129 acres of land, 10 acres of meadow, 16 acres of pasture, 1 acre wood and an acre of land and two messuages and two bovates of land in Clifton" were granted out to a new tenant. Thomas Boswell acquired the lot; the land having been seized into the lord's hands having had previously been held by Roche Abbey. The lands were said to have been held for "twelve years and longer" by the abbey without an entry fine (fee) having been paid, and therefore were subject to seizure.

The same year Tickhill and Conisbrough castle sites were surveyed for Henry VIII by three commissioners who returned this report (Tickhill omitted): "View of the castles of Tickhill and Conisbrough made by special commissioners 29 Henry VIII Jan 12th. Firstly the wooden and stone gates of the castle have fallen down. The bridge has fallen down. One round stone tower four storeys high and the tower width eight yards within the castle. In the first storey one well filled up with gravel. Other storeys are well repaired but one has fallen into decay with the value of twelve tons of timber and boards. The lead on the tower roof is decayed to the value of four, 151 and more. The walls have fallen between the said tower and the bridge for approximately sixty yards by estimation to a value of 151 and more. Stone walls within the castle and walls without the castle by estimation of 251 and more. All repairs within the castle and without, belonging to Wryte Warke by estimate of the value of the village of Conisbrough of 160 and more.
There is no artillery or ordinance in the said castle and no evidence of the horse mill there. There remains in the castle the lead gutters of the castle. Thomas Fairfax, Sergeant of Law; Thomas Green and Frances Frobisher"

"It's a bit crumbly but I'm sure it's safe enough"

The fallen walls that they described were due not to any attack on the castle, but to the instability of the natural subsoil of the hill on which the castle stands. Whereas the majority of the curtain wall had the natural rock outcrop of Middle Coal Measures sandstone as its foundation, a natural flaw in the rock left this part of the wall standing on sandstone and clay. The clay had dissolved over time and the foundation rock became very unstable and liable to crack. Eventually the whole of the hillside on the south side of the castle subsided in a catastrophic event. The subsidence had affected part of the barbican, the eastern turret of the gatehouse and part of its gate arch and the next tower eastwards.

Presumably the long list of repairs needed to make the castle viable again, especially the collapsed curtain wall, were just too big, and before long Henry VIII ordered the castellations to be taken down, making the castle undefendable. At some later date the remaining floors of the keep were burnt away in a massive fire.

In 1555 St Peter's started to record baptisms in a parish register and this was followed in 1559 with parish registers for Marriages and Burials which survive to the present day.

In 1559 the castle and all the Conisbrough estates were passed to Queen Elizabeth, who in turn passed them on to her cousin Henry Carey, who she had made first Lord Hunsdon. Carey was to hold the manor as her tenant-in-chief and it would remain in the Hunsdon family until the extinction of the male line. Sir Henry accompanied Elizabeth to Tilbury at the time of the Armada and played a prominent role over the years both at court and helping to protect the North from England's Scottish threat. Although he was created a baron, his ambition had been to become Earl of Wiltshire. The Queen visited him on his deathbed to grant him this earldom in 1596, but unimpressed by her last minute change of heart Henry was reported as saying, "Madam, seeing you counted me not worthy of this honour whilst I was living; I count myself unworthy of it now I am dying".

In 1581 Sir Edward Waterhouse of Halifax sold the whole of the Conisbrough Priory Manor formerly belonging to Lewes Priory, to Sir Arthur Ingram, Controller of Customs in the Port of London, though the Waterhouse family seem to have kept a stake in Conisbrough affairs. In 1612 a bequest from Richard Maxwell allowed a school to be set up in Conisbrough, and a further bequest a year later from Phillip Waterhouse, combined with Maxwell's to establish a grammar school for the village.

Conisbrough would continue in its pastoral role for the next few centuries, and despite the draining of the fens at Hatfield by Cornelius Vermuyden, diminishing the size of the Don, Conisbrough slowly built up its industrial heritage with Copley's iron works being established in 1645.

The following centuries saw Conisbrough adopting a non-fortified and peaceful role as a rural village centred on agriculture and small cottage industries. There are a few buildings dating back from the seventeenth and eighteenth century and these are of a characteristic building form found in the villages on the limestone belt around Doncaster. The underlying Magnesian limestone provides an excellent building material producing creamy stone buildings with clay pantile roofs. Before the use of pantiles, stone slates or thatch would have been used but there are no surviving examples today. 1645 was also the first year of the English Civil War, the struggle between King Charles and his Parliament. Conisbrough was not garrisoned due to its deterioration and the only evidence of the conflict in the village is superficial damage which was caused inside the church. The fate of Sandal Castle shows how fortunate we were that the curtain wall had collapsed. Sandal seems to have been left to deteriorate like Conisbrough from about 1600, but it was briefly re-fortified by a Royalist garrison during the Civil War. The occupation only lasted a few months but in 1646, on the orders of Parliament, the castle was stripped of its defences. The ruins of Tickhill, Pontefract, Sheffield, and Sandal castles are sobering examples of the thoroughness with which this order was carried out.

Conisbrough Castle and Estate remained in the Hunsdon family until the extinction of the male line, when Lady Mary Carey inherited it from her husband Pelham Carey. She subsequently married George Peyler, although she was always known as Lady Carey. Mary died very rich in 1696, and her property descended to her grand-daughter and heiress Carey Newton, who married Edward Coke, of Holkham in Norfolk.

A younger son of this marriage Edward Coke, inherited Conisbrough and on his death in 1737, the estate was sold to Thomas Osborne, fourth Duke of Leeds.

And this is where I will leave my history of Conisbrough, as a sleepy backwater waiting for its day in the sun again, when Sir Walter Scott would stir peoples' imagination about our picturesque castle, and start what was a boom time for Conisbrough from the1820s; before the collieries dominated the countryside, polluting the air, and Conisbrough started its new journey in time.

Glossary

Advowson-The right of a patron to present to the diocesan bishop a nominee for appointment to a vacant ecclesiastical benefice or church living

Agistment- The monetary proceeds of pasturing cattle in the king's forests

Alienated- sold without licence or a fee taken

Amercement- The penalty (fine) decided on by the court

Arras- a wall hanging made of rich tapestry used to conceal an alcove

Ashlar- Squared hewn stone laid in regular courses

Assize of Bread and Ale- Thirteenth century statute setting out quality control for those staples of the English diet

Attainted- The crime of the father wasn't passed on to the son

Barbican- Outer defence, protecting castle entrance

Battlement- Parapet with defensive indentations

BCE– Before the common era, previously BC

Bovate- Old land measurement which averaged around 20 English acres

Burgh- Fortified settlement usually surrounded by high earth banks

Capital- Uppermost part of a column

Castellations- Castle-like fortifications; battlements and crenellations

CE– Common era, previously AD

Chancelry- Part of the church where the alter and choir is

Chattel- All portable property of the tenant

Cist- Small stone-built coffin-like box

Clustered Column- Group of slender shafts joined to form a single column

Corbel- Projecting stone used as a support

Court leet, or tourn- A court of record held twice yearly in a lordship, or manor

Crenellation- Rampart around the top of a castle with regular gaps for firing arrows or guns

Curfews- Fire covers used to keep the embers of the fire overnight

Demesne- Land possessed or occupied by the owner himself

Demised- Grant an estate by will or lease

Dowager- A widow who holds a title or property derived from her deceased spouse

Escheator - A royal officer responsible for taking property of a person who has died without heirs to the crown

Fealty-An oath of fidelity promising not to harm his lord or to do damage to his property

Fee- Heritable estate in land

Fee tail-An entire estate which is handed down from eldest son to eldest son for as long as the bloodline continues

Flint microliths- small shaped flint items, typically arrows or spears

Fold-To place sheep in an enclosed area on a piece of ground, to manure it

Frankpledge-System under which peasants were bound together to keep the peace

Freeman- a person who is not a slave or serf

Fyrd- The local militia of an Anglo-Saxon shire, in which all freemen had to serve

Garrison– To put a group of soldiers in a place in order to live there and defend it

Gruel- A thinner version of porridge made out of some type of cereal boiled in water or milk

Hayward- Person responsible for maintaining hedges and fences so crops were not harmed

Heriot- A part of the feudal service: originally the return of a deceased tenant's military ware to a lord, but later the giving of the tenant's best live beast or chattel on his death

Inquisition- A legal or judicial inquiry to decide over a dispute in a civil or criminal case.

Joggled- Sideways 'Z' blocks held in place by notch to prevent slipping (of stonework)

Keep- Principal tower or stronghold of a castle

Lateral chamber-One storey extension to the porticus where the priest would change ready for services

Lintel- Horizontal beam or stone bridging doorway or opening

Haibot- The wood or thorns allowed to a tenant by law for repairing hedges or fences

Manumitted- Freed (of an indentured man)

Mesolithic- Middle Stone Age with chipped stone tools and more animal resources used

Messuage- A dwelling house, its outbuildings and adjacent land

Moot hall- Meeting or assembly building, traditionally used to decide local issues dating back to Anglo-Saxon times

Motte-and-Bailey- Early Norman castle style, consisting of palisaded courtyard enclosing steep mound topped with a wooden tower

Mullion- Vertical strut dividing window into lights and panes

Nave- Central aisle of a church; in this case the full width of the main congregation area

Neolithic- New Stone Age, less nomadic lifestyle, with polished stone tools and microliths

Oriel- A bay window projecting from an upper storey

Palaeolithic- Early phase of the Stone Age, when primitive stone implements were used

Palisade- Defensive palings of strong timber

Pannage- The right or privilege to pasture pigs (or other animals) in a forest

Pentice- Roofed lean-to, adjoining larger building or wall; a weather-protection

Pinfold– Stone built gated enclosure where strays were kept while their owner was found

Piscina- Shallow basin in wall of church, in which sacred vessels are washed

Portcullis- Heavy iron and wooden grating, lowered into gateway of castle from above

Porticus-Two storey part of a church jutting out of the side to give it the cross shape

Pottage- A thick soup or stew of vegetables, grains, and, if available, meat or fish

Primary- Book of readings from the Bible

Puritan iconoclasm- In the civil war in the 1640s puritans defaced statues in churches as idols and graven images

Quatrefoil- Tracery carved in the form of a four-lobed flower

Quo Warranto- Literally 'by what warrant?' By whose authority

Respite of service- Accepted breaks in a villein's obligatory service to the lord

Rib-Vaulted- Vault or ceiling supported by stone ribs, usually in a decorative way

Screens Passage- Entrance passage between a medieval hall and its service kitchens

Seisin- Denotes the legal possession of an estate in land

Serf- unfree peasant (also villein)

Smoother- the equivalent of a modern electric iron

State Room- a large room, in a castle, used for formal or important occasions

Stew- Fish pond used to store live fish ready for eating.

Tithe- one tenth of annual produce or earnings for the support of the Church

Trefoil- Tracery in the form of a three-lobed flower

Tumbrell- Right to erect and employ an instrument of punishment, ie pillory or ducking stool

Vault- An arched roof or ceiling

Vert- The green undergrowth which was needed to feed the beasts of the chase

View of frankpledge- The gathering and inspection in the court leet twice a year of all the men who were or ought to be in frankpledge

Villein- A peasant occupier entirely subject to a lord

Viscera- The soft internal organs of the body

Wassail- Spiced ale served with great ceremony at Christmas

Bibliography

Allport, CH. A History of Conisbrough
Anderson, OS. The English Hundred-Names
Arc Heritage. Doncaster Local Plan: Archaeological Scoping Assessment:
Barber, Brian. Manors and Manorial Records
Barton, Ingrid. The Little history of Yorkshire & The Vikings in Yorkshire
Batlett, Robert. England Under the Norman and Angevin Kings
Bennett-Connelly, Sharon. Defenders of the Norman Crown
Brindle, Steven and Agnieszka Sadraei. Conisbrough Castle
Buckland, Paul C. David Hey, Richard O'Neill, Ian Tyers. The Conisbrough Estate and the southern boundary of Northumbria.
Chadwick, A M Fields for Discourse: Landscape and Materialities of Being in South and West Yorkshire and Nottinghamshire during the Iron Age and Romano-British Periods.
Clay CT., Farrer W., Early Yorkshire Charters, Vol 8, The Honour of Warenne Conisbrough Manorial Court Rolls,
Inquisitions Post Mortem, Vol. II, Edward I, 633, p. 382.
Cockrell, Timothy Frank. Don Valley in Prehistory: Upland and Lowland Developments and Interactions
Connolly, Sharon Bennett. Conisbrough Castle – its Life and History; Gundrada de Warenne
Cowen, Brian and Canon GF Braithwaite. Conisbrough A short history
Dalton, Paul. Feudal Politics in Yorkshire 1066- 1154
Dannatt, FG. Conisbrough - The Ups and Downs of a Medieval Castle
Eddison, Edwin. History of Worksop; with sketches of Sherwood forest and the neighbourhood 1854
Ellis, HW. 'Conisbrough Castle', Yorkshire Archaeological Journal,
English Heritage Battlefield Report: Stamford Bridge 1066
English Heritage Teacher's pack
Fairbank, F. R. The Last Earl of Warenne and Surrey and the Distribution of his Possessions. YAJ
Gibbons, Kevin S. Hunting for Status: The Animal Bones from Conisbrough Castle and Cowick Manor, Yorkshire
Griffiths, JEA. A Knight in Conisbrough 1994
Hall, Richard The Jorvik Viking Centre- Houses
Hanson, Marilee.First Barons' War (1215 – 1217)
Harrison, S. Conisbrough Castle: An Initial Brief Review of the Architectural Problems and the Evidence of the Architectural Fragments
Hayfield, Colin and Paul Buckland. Late Medieval pottery wasters from Firsby, South Yorkshire
Historic England. Battle of Hastings
Holdsworth, David. Ivanhoe's Conisbrough
Horsfall Turner, Joseph. The History of Brighouse, Raistrick and Hipperholme
Hunter, Rev. Joseph 1825 Coningsborough An extract from the Deanery of Doncaster; Hameline, 5th Earl of Surrey
Johnson. Memoirs of the Ancient Earls of Warren and Surrey 1304-19 and 1326-47
Johnson, Stephen. Conisbrough Castle South Yorkshire
Jones, Dan. The Plantagenets
Köhler, Carl. A History of Costume 1928
Lloyd-Rees, Penny. Conisbrough and Denaby Industries through the ages
Matthew, Donald. King Stephen; Medieval Lands Project on the Earls of Surrey, Conisbrough Castle
Mattingly, H B and M J Dolby A Hoard of Barbarous Radiates and Associated Material from Sprotbrough, S Yorks
Morehouse, HJ. The History and Topography of the Parish of Kirkburton and of the Graveship of Holme (1861)
Morris, Dr Marc. The brutal story of the Harrying of the North
Pace, Edwin. Geoffrey's 'Very Old Book' and Penda of Mercia
Piponnier, Francoise, and Perrine Mane. Dress in the Middle Ages 1997
Planché, JR. The Conqueror and His Companions
Ryder PF. 1982 Saxon Churches in South Yorkshire
Salvagno L. The role of goat in English medieval husbandry and economy
Sands, Harold and Hugh Braun. Conisbrough and Mortemer
Shepperson, Tessa. A confusion of courts
Smith, William. Castle description and history
Sturlason, Snorri. The Heimskringla Saga
Thompson, M W. Further work at Conisburgh Castle, Yorkshire

Vitalis, Odericus. Historia Ecclesiastica
Walker, Kathryn. Illegitimate Children of John de Warenne
Wood, Rita. The Romanesque Memorial at Conisbrough
Yorkshire Archaeological Journal Vol 52 1980

Calendar of Chancery Warrants 1244-1326
Calendar of Patent Rolls XII/1 507.
Charter of Ethelred II confirming the grant by Wulfric Spot of possessions in Staffordshire, Derbyshire and Warwickshire for the foundation of Burton Abbey, 1004
Mexborough & Swinton Times, March 14 1923 Conisborough Castle by Ivanhoe
Mexborough and Swinton Times July 9, 1926 Excavation at Conisborough Castle
Notes on Old Conisbrough by Doncaster Library Service 1985
St Peter's Church Leaflet

https://academic.oup.com/book/1457/chapter-abstract/140846379
https://adventuresofatudornerd.com/2018/08/15/biography-richard-duke-of-york/
http://www.ancientfortresses.org/
https://www.andalucia.com/history/monarchs-of-castile
https://aprilmunday.wordpress.com/2019/03/03/medieval-linen/
https://archaeologydataservice.ac.uk/
https://archive.org/stream/YASWCR003/YASWCR003_djvu.txt// yorkshirearchae14socigoog/page/221/mode/2up?view=theater William Brown
www.arild-hauge.com/ Arild Hauge's Runes
https://www.bbc.co.uk/news/health-63316538 Black Death
http://www.berkshirehistory.com/articles/earls_revolt.html
https://www.bow-international.com/features/traditional/old-archery-games/
https://www.bmc-historyandheritage.co.uk/
https://brewminate.com/ Middle Eastern History
https://brigantesnation.com/
https://www.britainexpress.com/ The Council of the North
https://www.google.co.uk/books/edition/Britannic_Researches
https://www.british-history.ac.uk/vch/surrey/vol4/pp135-151/ vch/sussex/vol7/pp1-7 / /inquis-post-mortem/vol18/pp294-308// inquis-post-mortem/vol18/pp308-324// inquis-post-mortem/vol18/pp294-308// cal-treasury-books/vol4/pp678-689
https://conisbroughanddenabyhistory.org.uk/
https://www.conisbroughcastle.org.uk/lords-of-the-manor/
https://sites.google.com/site/conisbroughlocalhistory/court-rolls/surveyor-of-the-highways
https://www.dhi.ac.uk/conisbrough/specimen_1349-50// cistercians/roche/
http://www.domesdaybook.co.uk/
https://doncasterhistory.wordpress.com
http://www.earlybritishkingdoms.com/
https://www.english-heritage.org.uk/visit/places/conisbrough-castle/history/Yorkshire//earn/histories/dissolution/
https://englishhistory.net/middle-ages/the-normans/
https://erenow.net/postclassical/crusades/839.php
https://etheses.whiterose.ac.uk/ Theses Online
https://www.domesdaybook.net/ Hull Doomsday Project
http://www.facesofarthur.org.uk/fabio/book6.7b.htm
https://www.familysearch.org/en/wiki/England_Militia_History
https://www.geni.com/people/Maud-de-Nerford// Isabella-of-Castile-Duchess-consort-of-York// Maud-de-Clifford-Countess-of-Cambridge/
https://www.gethistory.co.uk/historical-period/ancient/roman/julius-caesars-invasion-of-britain
https://www.haxeywalkers.co.uk/linen-and-hemp-in-the-isle/
https://sites.google.com/site/haydonhaydenkeysgenealogy/william-de-warren-the-conqueror-and-his-companions

G:\Heritage Day\Research\Conisbrough History\Ancient History\Anglo Saxon Conisbrough\Ancient Peoples in

https://www.heritagedoncaster.org.uk

https://historicengland.org.uk/research/results/reports/8598/ ConisbroughCastleSouthYorkshire_AnalyticalEarthworkSurvey

https://www.historyfiles.co.uk/

https://www.historynet.com/last-stand-ely/

http://historyoflaw.co.uk/

http://historyofthorne.com/peel_hill.html

www.history.org.uk/primary/resource/3860/teaching-romans-anglo-saxons-and-vikings-in-brit

https://historytheinterestingbits.com//earl-warenne-and-the-second-crusade// maud-clifford// Isabella of Castile//

https://historylearning.com/medieval-england/the-crusades/second-crusade/

http://www.hrionline.ac.uk/conisbrough/index.html

https://www.humanrights.com/what-are-human-rights/brief-history/magna-carta.html

https://inquisitionspostmortem.ac.uk/view/inquisition/18-861/862

https://www.kent-opc.org/opcfamilydata

  https://kids.britannica.com/students/article/Middle-Ages/275833

https://kirkleescousins.co.uk/early-days/ Ancient peoples in Yorkshire

https://leweshistory.org.uk/

https://lewespriory.org.uk/history-overview

https://www.lindleyancestry.com/old_conisbrough.htm

https://localhistories.org/tudor-houses/

https://www.lse.ac.uk/research/research-for-the-world/economics/lords-of-the-manor-feudal-law-and-its-impact-on-rural-village-life

https://www.luminarium.org/encyclopedia/edwardyork.htm

https://www.medievalists.net/2022/12/scientific-facts-black-death/ medieval-military-revolution/ charter -forest/

http://medievaljames.blogspot.com/2011/03/medieval-basket-making.html

https://www.medieval-life-and-times.info/medieval-life/medieval-archer.htm

www.megalithic.co.uk/article.php?sid=26833

https://mexboroughheritage.wordpress.com/

http://midgleywebpages.com/index-3.html //stewards.html

 http://warrenfamilyhistory.com/

http://wasleys.org.uk/eleanor/churches

https://www.wealddown.co.uk/course-news/flax-processing/

https://weavingword.wordpress.com/2016/06/13/medieval-monday-turning-flax-into-linen/

www.werelate.org

https://en.wikipedia.org/wiki/Ambrosius Aurelianus// Battle of Lincoln// John de Warenne,6th Earl of Surrey// Edward, 2nd Duke of York// Earl of Surrey// Lewes Castle// Philippa Mohun// Wakefield Castle//William de Warenne, 3rd Earl of Surrey// Richard of Conisburgh, 3rd Earl of Cambridge// Conisbrough Castle and its incumbrants

ttps://mortimerhistorysociety.org.uk/

https://www.nationalarchives.gov.uk/help-with-your-research/research-guides/medieval-early-modern-soldiers

https://www.nature.com/articles/s41586-022-05349-x

https://www.newforestnpa.gov.uk/app/uploads/2018/03/history1_medieval.pdf

https://www.on-magazine.co.uk/yorkshire/history/the-romans-in-yorkshire/ By Ingrid Barton

https://pontefractsandalcastles.org.uk/thomas-of-lancaster-saint-or-sinner// pontefract-castle-15th-century/

https://www.quora.com/ Crusades

https://www.researchgate.net/publication/234037890_Conisbrough_with_figures

https://researchframeworks.org/syrf/later-medieval/?highlight=conisbrough

http://www.roman-britain.co.uk/tribes/coritani/

www.royal.uk William the Conqueror

https://schoolshistory.org.uk/topics/british-history/normans/odo-of-bayeux/
https://www.search.staffspasttrack.org.uk
www.tha-engliscan-gesithas.org.uk The English Companions
https://www.thehistorypress.co.uk/articles/the house of york edmund of Langley and his children/
https://www.thetimetravellers.org.uk/brigantes-group.html
https://www.thoughtco.com/medieval-food-preservation-1788842
https://www.wakefield.gov.uk/museums-and-castles/sandal-castle-history
https://www.wikitree.com/ 6th earl de Warenne
https://www.worldhistory.org/Richard Duke of York//timeline/Wars of the Roses/
https://www.yas.org.uk/ Wakefield Manor Court Rolls Vol. 03

Postscript

Our Castle

Strong, silent sentinel, keep of stone
Historic castle, of defence grey to age
Matured to nature's mood, defied alone
Erect and proud, persevered stormy rage
Set in rock, man's folly to tolerate
Thy beauty breathes alive traditional scene
Thy vallum withstood, furious foes all abate
The glory of Conisbrough, thy presence redeem.

Designed of man, deemed forbidding cold
Thy crown seem kiss, unhurried white cloud
Old image now warm, ancient charm unfold
Perfect thy setting, yet mystery enshroud
In splendour reign thy panoramic rule
Ravaged in bygone war and confrontation
Arid thy moat, dancing trout once pool
Portals now ajar, doth welcome all nation.

Did holy being mark thy pleasant place
On mound aloof, to gaze on flowing Don
Akin Mill Piece, nestles snug of verdant face
Rekindle our thoughts, of age long gone
Doth knight of past thy precinct's ghost
Thy greens full courts, amuse to jesters' fun
Our heritage preserved, town's birth you host
Then pray you stand, till death of sun.

Plantagenets and Tudors, thou did survive
Chronicled events, to thy record did chart
Plague of Black, and God's laws revised
Thou stood time's test, derelict and apart
How humble we stand, to stony might
Thy silhouette outlined to beam of moon
Or thy monument, archives relate a noble plight
May future mankind, thy existence e'er groom.

Benny Wilkinson